ALL THE LOVING WOLVES

ALL
THE
LOVING
WOLVES

LIVING AND LEARNING
WITH WOLF HYBRIDS

Michael Belshaw

R · E · D
CRANE
BOOKS

First Edition

Printed in the United States of America

Photographs by Murrae Haynes
Illustrations by Jody King
Design by Joanna Hill

ISBN: 1-878610-02-3.
Library of Congress Catalog Card Number: 90-61683

Red Crane Books
826 Camino De Monte Rey
Santa Fe, New Mexico 87501

To wolves
To their wolf hybrid cousins
To those who seek to understand them
That from each other
We may learn

CONTENTS

Wolf hybrids are especially alert; they miss nothing.

PREFACE

In recent years, the American public has become fascinated by the wolf, an animal whose very name once struck the hearer with fear and revulsion. This interest has been accompanied by a wish on the part of many people to own such an animal, the better to become acquainted with it. The realization of this wish is thwarted by difficulties, both practical and legal, and so the wolf hybrid—part wolf, part dog—has become, as a surrogate wolf, a member of many households.

This unusual animal, delightful though he or she may be, requires a very different kind of care and attention than the domestic dog. The main purpose of this book is to guide people into harmony with the wolf hybrid should they choose to live with one. Above all, this harmony calls for a thorough understanding of the animal himself, which this book, drawing upon my long and close experience with hybrids, is designed to provide.

Although in the pages that follow the discussion is primarily about wolf hybrids, when talking of my own animals I sometimes refer to them as "wolves," rather than "wolf hybrids." This is mainly a convenience; but since each is more wolf than domestic dog, the characterization is neither misleading nor wholly inaccurate.

ALL THE LOVING WOLVES

INTRODUCTION:
GETTING INVOLVED

 "How did you get involved with WOLVES?" is a question very frequently directed to me. And the honest response to this is, "By accident."

I had been trapped in the numbing lockstep of an academic career for many years before I managed to settle in the West. Until the realization of that dream, I had inhabited such places as New Zealand, New York City and Connecticut, in none of which is *Canis lupus* normally an important element in one's consciousness. Since I did not think of wolves at all, I had few conceptions, or misconceptions, about them.

The first wolves I saw belonged to a colleague at Prescott College in Arizona where, during some of its short life, I was the entire Department of Economics. They were chained, clearly unloved, and were extremely nervous and uncomfortable with visitors. Frankly, it was hard to be favorably impressed by those poor creatures.

One of my other colleagues at the college was Jay Dusard, who has since found his calling as an eminent photographer of cowboys. One day in 1977 Jay called me for help. "Was driving to Copper Basin today behind this hippie flatbed. A dog fell off and they was too stoned to stop. I rescued him a bit dazed. He's real nice, but we got a helluva herd of dogs now. Can you take him?"

By this time, Prescott College had folded and I agreed to take the dog because Chucho, my German Shepherd, needed company during those long days when I was in Phoenix, employed in Arizona State Planning. I was impressed by the animal and soon realized that he was no common or garden variety of dog. He exhibited a much higher level of energy, a nurturance and loyalty to my family of cats, and a clear need to establish dominance over Chucho. It slowly dawned on me that his behavior and appearance were wolf-like and so I named him Lobo. Soon after, Chucho died of a heart attack and now it was Lobo who was left alone during my long absences in Phoenix. Eventually he went A.W.O.L. from lonesomeness, but by that time I was hooked. And so, when I left Arizona for New Mexico, I took with me a small pack of wolf hybrids: Chula, Chaco and Chamaco.

My experience of pure wolves remains limited to those of my former colleague and a few that I have stared at in zoos. Now and again I have seen captive or tame representatives in other settings, but never in a situation that allowed anything more than a brief, and not very satisfying, acquaintance. The interest aroused by Lobo led me to read all the books and articles on wolves that I could lay my hands on. I especially appreciated the works of R. D. Lawrence, who is, one might say, an experiential naturalist—one who by intimate observation seeks to fathom deeply what he observes.

Once, and only once, have I seen a wolf in the wild, and that not very far from where this is written. One early June day a friend and I were exploring some mountains. We noticed some sheep, shorn of their winter coat, that had just been let out to pasture. Then a white canid jumped into the dirt road ahead of us, disappearing as soon as there was mutual recognition. It stayed just long enough for me to note, by its conformation, that it either was a monster *Canis latrans* (coyote) or a smallish *Canis lupus* (wolf). Certainly he (or she, more likely) was intending to mingle with the flock of sheep in a manner clearly to their disadvantage.

This animal, or another like it, has since been observed close-to by others, including a horseman riding high in those same mountains. Officially, wild wolves are said not to exist in New Mexico, since some brutal extermination by "conservationists" that persisted into the 'thirties. Although I am sympathetic to cattle and sheep owners, who hardly need another obstacle to their livelihood, I find myself rooting for that white wolf, a symbol of American wildlife that should survive.

Since owning feral or captive wolves is impracticable, I have opted for wolf hybrids. I became involved in breeding so that I might share with others the delights of intimacy, love and companionship that derive from the complex interaction that takes place.

What lies behind this strong upsurge of interest throughout the country in owning wolf hybrids? Hybrids have associated with human beings since before recorded time, and native peoples such as the Eskimo have long bred their domesticated dogs to wild wolves. Defined breeds, such as Huskies, Malamutes and German Shepherds, are believed to have strong

Chicha demonstrates bonding and affection.

wolf elements. Hybrids have served man in sled teams, and in this capacity they assisted the scientific explorations of Admiral Richard Byrd. But the rise in popularity of wolf hybrids as domestic pets and companions is a relatively recent phenomenon. Why?

It is possible that the interest was latent and only needed some catalyst to make the demand effective. Many visitors to my ranch have made some such statement as, "I've always wanted to own a wolf, but didn't know how to do it." Or, "My family had a dog that we thought was part wolf and I'll never forget him."

The change in attitude towards such animals may be due to the increased environmental sensitivity of recent years. Now that the world is in danger of losing much of its natural habitat—wild, untouched and profoundly meaningful to man—we have come to appreciate its significance. We seek ways to sustain the connection, and intimacy with half-feral creatures can be one of them.

Popular books and movies, such as *The Journey of Natti Gann* and *Never Cry Wolf*, misleading in some respects though they may be, have stimulated an awareness of the wolf that is quite different from that fostered by ignorance. Traditional perceptions are expressed when people ask, "Is he mean? Aren't you afraid of him? Won't he turn on you when he gets older?" But I encounter these attitudes less often than a fascinated curiosity and desire to make some connection with the animals. Wolf hybrids must do something special for some of us. Why else would we willingly go to the expense and unusual effort involved in owning them?

There are some people whose reasons may not be of the best, who have an overwhelming need to attract attention to themselves, irrespective of how this may affect the exotic animal vehicle they use—be it wolf, mountain lion, monkey or macaw. Individuals with such unbalanced egos do not make good owners of sensitive animals like wolf hybrids. Other people are inspired by fear to purchase wolf hybrids for guard and protection duty. As we shall see later, they are not as well suited to these purposes as domestic dogs. Now and again an aspiring mountain man shows up at my ranch looking for a wolf hybrid to be his alter ego, roaming by his side through the forests and mountain passes. Sometimes this will work, but large domesticated canids that run free are, as we shall see later, a recipe for tragedy.

Wolf hybrids legitimately excite the curiosity of people who find domestic breeds a trifle bland. Looking for something more challenging, they are impressed by the vitality and strong personalities of the wolf hybrids. People who own these animals do not often go back to owning dogs.

In what characteristics lie their special charm? Wolf hybrids exhibit complex intelligence, extraordinary lightness and grace, and an apparent awareness of things in their surroundings that elude man. Some people claim to perceive in them a mystical quality. Mine have been used in healing ceremonies and seem to have helped to restore damaged souls.

If one is privileged to live with a pack of hybrid wolves, the intricacies and subtleties of their social system are a challenge to interpret and understand. In my case, this has led to an enhanced understanding of human social structure and needs, and has helped me to understand and alter aspects of my own behavior, not a few of which were in need of modification.

Chamaco, an alpha male, responds to a guest.

One of the delights of ownership, especially of a pack, comes when the songs begin. Hearing the wolf songs is an experience so profound, so powerful, so moving, that all else is held in suspension. One experiences a rare privilege and is witness to a ceremony that goes far beyond the limits of human understanding.*

The costs of breeding wolf hybrids are great, but even more so are the extraordinary efforts required of a single individual who has no help in this task. I must be home to feed the animals twice a day, and to meet with clients, and these demands severely restrict the normal freedoms of social transactions and travel to distant places. Initially I wanted to share with others the pleasure of these animals, and, in so doing, at least cover my costs. But very few breeders of any animal, be it wolves, dogs, cats, or horses, make a living at the enterprise.

As time progressed, my motives became more complex and more personal. As I lived more closely with my growing pack I became fascinated by their family bonds and individual personalities, and deeply impressed by their integrity and a mystical quality I have yet to fully understand. As more and more visitors arrived, I realized, too, that a mission was evolving, a responsibility to the interests and survival of the wolf in the wild, strongly shared by many of the people who come to the ranch to see my pack. Warm friendships have developed with buyers and non-buyers alike, as we share our appreciation for these animals that have brought us together.

But there is another aspect, inevitable but not easy to

---

*Too often, when there are visitors at my ranch and the wolves begin to howl, someone will destroy the mood by asking, "Why are they doing that?" How shattering can be the babble of human tongues!

accept. As I write this, my heart lies heavy for little Quiver who died two days ago as the result of an automobile accident. Quiver, the light-colored daughter of Atsay, had meant so much to Alice, her owner and friend. Together they had explored the mountain trails of the Sangre de Cristos and ventured into the spiritual paths unique to wolves and their accepted allies. Animals must die and we know this. But the grief is hardly bearable at times.

1

WOLVES AND WOLF HYBRIDS

When we read the literature on wolves, it is clear that little is known of this animal, much studied as it is. There are many contradictory opinions, especially as to pack size and whether wolves are a threat to man.

In one respected publication the assertion had been made that wolves run with raised tails, in contrast to the coyote which runs with the tail straight down. A popular field guide* states that the tail of the coyote "is *held down* between the hind legs *when running.*" For the wolf, "when running, the *tail is carried high*" and red wolves run "with their *tails out behind.*" One might interpret this to mean that wolves carry their tails *over their backs* when running, in the fashion of Malamutes and Huskies. But the facts of the matter are more complex.

---

*W. H. Burt and R. P. Grossenheider, *A Field Guide to the Mammals: The Peterson Field Guide Series*, sponsored by the National Audubon Society and National Wildlife Federation, and published by Houghton Mifflin, Boston, Fifth Printing, 1959, pp. 51, 52. Italics in original.

The general tendency is for wolves, when running or trotting, to carry their tails streaming behind, slightly below the horizontal. However, the *alpha* wolf in the lead may carry his tail higher, rather like a flag. The reason for this became clear to me once when my pack was trotting through the chaparral. All that could be seen from a distance was the tail of the *alpha*, seemingly carrying the flag for the others to follow. Tail posture is variable, and specific meanings, such as confidence, threat or abject submission, are clearly conveyed by it. This subject is well addressed in books by David Mech and Erik Zimen.*

The wolf has an awesome reputation, engendering fear in many people. Yet recorded attacks in North American wilds are few (see Chapter Six, *Myths*). The many inaccurate ideas about this animal reflect our limited opportunities to observe it and the animal's environmental adaptation.

In part because of the wide territory through which it ranges, zoologists studying the wolf in the wild cannot do so continuously, and so only fragments of its lifeway are observed. The behavior of the captive wolf is, necessarily, altered. In captivity, he no longer has to hunt for his prey, and his territory and freedom of movement are severely constrained. This is true of my pack; and the generality of my observations on wolves is further limited by the admixture with the dog. Nevertheless, hybrids exhibit enough wolf–like characteristics for their behavior to be enormously instructive.

*L. David Mech, *The Wolf: The Ecology and Behavior of an Endangered Species,* Natural History Press, Garden City, N.Y., 1970, p. 83; and Erik Zimen, *The Wolf: His Place in the Natural World*, Souvenir Press, London, 1981, pp. 58, 59 and 63.

Because the wolf, as a species, is so widely dis-
tributed, a variety of environmental parameters will
affect its habits. Clear examples of this kind of variation are not readily available from the literature. However, this point is illustrated by using the blue fox as an
example. M. L. Washburn, a member of the Harriman
expedition to Alaska, wrote an article on fox farming,
and noted some interspecies behavioral differences.

> A marked difference exists between the habits of foxes on
> St. Paul and St. George islands and materially affects the
> question of their cultivation. On St. George they flock
> around the village in winter and seize greedily any articles
> of food lying about and, as previously noted, are quite tame
> and readily handled in the large wire cage. On St. Paul they
> are rarely seen about the village and the carcasses of mules
> dying in the winter have remained untouched. Nor has it
> been possible to induce them to congregate at any fixed
> place, even by scattering dried fish about. The result is that
> although much study has been given the matter, no systen
> has yet has been devised of cultivating the foxes or of han-
> dling them on St. Paul Island except by using steel traps,
> which destroy male and female alike; this necessitates
> limiting the catch so as not to encroach too closely on the
> breeding stock. The difference in habits on the two islands
> presents a problem which has not yet been solved, nor has
> the further fact been explained fully that although on St.
> George Island the foxes have received an abundance of food
> and the females have been carefully protected, there has
> been no appreciable increase; on the contrary, as compared
> with olden times, there has been a diminution.*

The explanation for the last noted phenomenon is
obvious. When animals are not promiscuous and mate
for life, the destruction of the males leaves the females

*M. L. Washburn, "Habits of foxes on Pribiloff Islands," in John Bur-
roughs, John Muir, et al., *Alaska: The Harriman Expedition, 1899*, Dover,
N.Y., 1986, p. 363.

A three-month-old female cub.

without the nurturance of their natural and beloved mates.

This quotation highlights the fact that unexplained differences can exist within subgroups of a species at a given time. As to wolves, they are found in diverse habitats—Arctic tundra, open steppes and plains, high mountains, deep forests, deserts and subtemperate islands—and this ecological diversity undoubtedly has led to diverse adaptations. For example, while a large pack is required for the cooperative hunting of caribou or buffalo, many of the prey in mountain areas, such as whitetail deer, can be handled by only two or three wolves.

The wolf does not have the reputation for adaptability of the coyote, which has invaded semi-urbanized areas. However, recent reports of possible sightings of wolves in the Southwest raise the possibility that their adaptability might be greater than formerly supposed. Most of the sightings have been of single animals, although one, in Arizona's White Mountains, was of five. Is it possible that, because of the vulnerability of large packs to human predation, the wolf adapted by abandoning the pack for smaller nuclear family groups; or have mountain-based wolves, such as those in the sightings, always operated in small numbers? The latter position is favored in *The Wolf of the Southwest*.

> Available data suggest that large packs (of six or more wolves) were rare here, which seems reasonable since their natural prey were individual deer. The evolution to large pack behavior would render these conditions a liability rather than an asset. Small-scale social organization appeared to persist even after the advent of large domestic prey; almost all actual accounts were of single animals, pairs, and small packs of family groups or siblings.*

Differences of opinion on this and other specific questions of wolf behavior reflect the difficulty in making assertions and generalizations about wolves and their way of life.

Hybrids Defined

A wolf hybrid is the result of interbreeding between a wolf and some other canid, usually a domestic dog, or between two wolf hybrids perhaps several generations removed from the pure wolf. Breeders in the United States show a strong preference for interbreeding wolves and Malamutes, although other dog inputs are sometimes found. It is generally believed that the

*David E. Brown, ed., *The Wolf of the Southwest—The Making of an Endangered Species,* University of Arizona Press, Tucson, 1983, pp. 140-141.

Malamute is a native breed developed by the Mahlemat Indians and derived from the Husky with infusions of the wolf. Whatever the case, the Malamute exhibits considerable behavioral similarity to the wolf, but mellows out some of the wolf's wariness. However, the Malamute's forward curving tail, probably necessary and desirable in a sled animal, is quite different from that of the wolf, whose tail tends to flow behind and to be held horizontal when in motion. Brown eyes, common to the Malamute, are quite rare among wild wolves, whose eyes typically are light in color. The brown eyes, recurved tail and heavier body structure of the Malamute are common indications of the dog element in a wolf hybrid.

German Shepherds, also believed to be close lineal descendants of wolves, are sometimes crossed with them. Although the tail of the German Shepherd is carried in a manner similar to that of the wolf, the ears are much larger and set closer together, and the head is more massive. A dark muzzle and a black body saddle often indicate the German Shepherd influence in a wolf hybrid but may originate with other breeds. Temperamentally, the German Shepherd is more wary than the Malamute, and the resultant hybrid can accentuate characteristics that many breeders want to avoid. However, quarter–wolf German Shepherd crosses have been bred specifically for guard and protection training. The wolf element in the gene pool may also protect against the German Shepherd's tendency toward hip dysplasure, a crippling degeneration of the hind quarters.

Why Not Own a Pure Wolf?

The ownership of pure wolves is restricted by federal and state laws, in part for their protection as an endan-

Fantasma shows the long-legged gait that allows wolves to cover long distance with ease.

gered species, but also because pure wolves are not easily constrained by the limitations of human society and ecology. An animal of *Canis familiaris* descent, such as the Malamute, leavens wolf behavior in such a way, and to such a degree, that we have an animal that can adapt itself satisfactorily to our lifeways. Yet it retains many of the characteristics of pure wolves that we find so attractive.

Although an individual pure wolf may be as tractable and mellow as a domestic dog, this is probably the exception. Pure wolves, for reasons easily understood, are wary of human beings and are not relaxed around us. They protect their interests by staying out of our way, and while some may accept and trust their owners and keepers, they usually are extremely cautious when confronted by other people. This is not an especially relaxing situation and is not conducive to socialization and companionship.

The Malamute, on the other hand, is easily socialized and demonstrative. Except for the physical characteristics mentioned earlier, his contribution to a wolf hybrid is most compatible with the wolf element.

Characteristics of Wolves and Wolf Hybrids

Some authorities believe that wolves, and by extension wolf hybrids, have many attributes in common with a basic unit of mankind, the extended family. In the United States, unless we live near stable groups of traditional peoples, we are hardly aware of the extended family. We may be ignorant of the high degree of social integration and the warm supportiveness it can afford; or we may view it with some degree of envy. Living with wolf hybrids makes it possible for us to experience, or at least observe, some elements of this close interaction of the extended family group.

The largest functioning social unit among wolves is the pack, which can number from three to more than 20 animals. The principal function of the pack is economic. The wolf often preys on animals much larger than itself and the combined efforts of several wolves are needed to bring down a moose or a buffalo. By contrast the coyote, for example, a canid only one-third the size of the wolf, even with help would experience extreme difficulty with large prey. Consequently the coyote pursues smaller animals, such as rabbits, which do not require the hunting cooperation of several other animals. A pair of coyotes can handle the situation quite nicely, thank you.

Hope Ryden, in her classic *God's Dog*, amplifies this distinction for us.

> As suitors, coyotes may even outshine wolves. At least, pair bonding appears more visible in coyotes, but perhaps this is only because intense pack affiliation does not obscure it. For though the coyote does exhibit allegiance to a few pack members, he is by no means no [sic] group oriented as the wolf. On the contrary, the coyote's primary social unit seems to be the pair, not the pack.
>
> Since pack affiliation has no great survivial value in the smaller coyote, who feeds primarily on small rodents and carrion, his first allegiance is to his mate. Perhaps to reinforce this intrinsic loyalty, Nature has made the male coyote as cyclical as the female.*

Wolves and coyotes are opportunists and they will eat whatever is tasty and available. As omnivores, they supplement meat with berries and other vegetable matter. Coyotes in the Southwest consume large amounts of juniper berries. My wolf hybrids greatly enjoy melons and will try to corner the market on any cantaloupes or watermelons I heave into the pens.

Wolves have another need imprinted within them that greatly facilitates pack hunting and which makes the wolf hybrids especially delightful to own. They are highly social animals. They crave companionship and are miserable without it. A "lone wolf" is a sorry, unhappy, dejected character—not to be compared with the macho chest–thumpers who characterize themselves as "lone wolves."

The social structure of the pack, then, has two distinguishing and mutually reinforcing traits. Wolves survive as a social unit by hunting together; and the social unit meets the strong emotional needs of the pack members.

*Hope Ryden, *God's Dog: A Celebration of the North American Coyote*, Penguin Books, Middlesex, England, 1979, pp. 68, 69.

Successful hunting is not a random affair. Some degree of coordination and role specialization is needed to develop and effectuate strategies. The pack requires leadership and hierarchy. Leadership is provided by the *alpha* wolves, the chiefs, as it were. The rest of the pack are *betas*—warriors.

Alpha and *beta* are unfortunately confusing and inadequate terms. *Alpha* might simply refer to a leadership position. But it is also used to characterize personality. An *alpha* personality tends to be aggressive, wary and reserved. But this individual might not be playing an *alpha* role in the pack, since he or she may yet be a yearling cub.

A *beta* could be a mellow fellow who is thoroughly willing to flow with life and get on with everyone. On the other hand, through accident or other circumstance, it is not impossible for a *beta* personality to play an *alpha* role and lead the pack. Complicating the matter further is the complex personality of the wolf. An animal may show *alpha* traits in certain aspects of its behavior, such as in dominance over other males, but may be thoroughly *beta* when it is transacting with humans—or with one particular human. Some may exhibit *beta* behavior, but temporarily become more aggressive, for example in seizing an opportunity to join in a fight to beat up an *alpha* who is temporarily down.

Roles within the pack are not rigidly fixed. Pack survival requires good leadership, but roles can be reversed. I have noted this especially among my females. If one of them is overbearing for too long, another will wait for a moment of weakness and take the opportunity to surprise the poop out of the erstwhile *alpha*. The tension is not often resolved without someone getting a severe thrashing.

To no small degree, a pack has a corporate character. Not only does it operate as a unit, despite individual personalities, but it is also self–perpetuating. Cubs are born into it every year—but usually only to the *alpha* male and *alpha* female. In the wild, these two exercise a demographic control over the entire pack, so that pack size and the availability of prey are in a rough, dynamic equilibrium. The *alpha* female protects her interests in breeding by preventing lower order females from mating.

The breeding season is a time of tensions within the pack and also for the breeder of wolf hybrids. Not only do the males have an understandable interest in the female who is in *estrus*, but the females become very competitive, and this is a time when an established order of wolves can be upset. The female who is mating becomes aggressive towards others and, if she has had a subordinate status previously, this may now be over- turned. Females who had previously gotten along famously can become permanent enemies. When they encounter each other, hackles are raised, lips curl, low growls are heard, and pushing and shoving ensues. The new female *alpha* may attack and knock down the established *alpha*, who is much suprised at this reversal.

Soon the males become agitated and a battle starts among them in which old scores are settled. When the dust settles, the old order may have changed and a new structure evolved. Pity the poor breeder whose wolf hybrid pack is battling, with bloody wounds and loud screams and fearsome growls. How does he stop the slaughter?

After the mating is accomplished things begin to set- tle down, but the owner or breeder must use great care

Mariah! is almost pure wolf, shy but gentle.

and tact to keep tensions from erupting again. Sometimes especially antagonistic pairs may have to be separated.

Problems such as these are less likely if breeding is prevented. In a pack in which all the females are spayed at an early age, erotic tensions may be deflected and a stable hierarchy established. Peace and joy can be one's reward!

Despite the violent behavior just discussed, it is neither inconsistent nor inaccurate to state that wolves have very nuturant personalities. They adore the cubs, and often other baby animals, especially human ones. The entire pack contributes to the welfare of the cubs. For example, pack members bring food to the mother while she is nursing, and will regurgitate meat so that she can feed. As the cubs grow and are weaned, they learn to trigger the regurgitating behavior of adults by licking and nuzzling the corners of his or her mouth. This is one of the behavioral manifestations that can carry over into adolescence and even adulthood. A subordinate animal will demonstrate his lower status by licking the mouth of a superior while crouching low on his hind legs and wagging his tail rapidly. He can be very persistent in this, sometimes to the annoyance of the animal subject to the attention. He, or she, will bear with it for awhile, assuming an air of indifference which may turn to irritation. The session can end with growls and a snap, and, if the dominant animal becomes especially provoked, he will knock the *beta* down.

Demonstrative behavior of this kind is characteristic of wolves and wolf hybrids. They derive great pleasure from licking those whom they like. A human can expect to be licked in the mouth insistently and end-lessly. Most of us, while appreciating the loving attention, would prefer that it take a different form.

In a hybrid breeding situation, it is usual to have more than one set of breeding partners in the pack. When humans assume the economic function of the pack, the need for the entire unit to support the cubs no longer exists. For example, one rarely sees cubs successfully persuading adults to regurgitate their food.

To understand both the wolf and the wolf hybrid, it helps to be aware of two conflicting behavioral characteristics that control the animal's reactions. These canids are, simultaneously, highly curious and very cautious.*

*Stan and Nancy Noyes of Santa Fe observed the same dichotomy in their wolf hybrid, Shiska. They noticed that when company came to the house Shiska was both scared and fascinated. She would watch the festivities for hours on end—but from a secure place beneath the dining room table.

The curiosity manifests in many ways. Wild wolves, for instance, are said to be attracted to the nighttime fires of travellers in the woods. My hybrids are always highly alert to visitors arriving and do not relax until they have been introduced. As an aside, I might note that they do not usually advise me of the arrival of visitors by vocalizing. However, if I happen to be watching the wolves, and notice them fixing their attention on a side canyon across the arroyo, a car or truck will appear within about ten minutes.

For wolves, anything new, animate or inanimate, merits investigation in hopes that it is something to play with or to eat. Whatever it is will, however, be treated with great caution until it is understood. This can be illustrated by my effort to introduce a new plaything into a pen in the form of an old truck tire. When I rolled it through the gate, the three wolves inside scattered to the farthest fence, then turned and watched intensely. After the tire rolled to a stop and lay flat on the ground, they approached it carefully, sniffed it and urinated on it. Eventually finding it wanting in interest, they separated, going back to where they had been before.

Clearly these opposing needs within the wolf are functional. Caution—concealment or flight—are essential to survival. Flight is preferred to fight. Intelligent curiosity also affords the wolf opportunities to discover something edible or, perhaps, amusing, for wolves are playful animals. Owners of wolf hybrids, especially of high percentage animals, are constantly reminded of this caution/curiosity syndrome. Even though a wolf or hybrid may have spent its entire life with this one human being, its caution and alertness will scarcely diminish. For example, if I enter Mariah!'s pen wearing a hat she has not seen before, or if I run

rather than walk, off she skitters to a far corner of the
enclosure until I prove that I am really me. Mariah!
usually greets me by jumping on a table, to make herself better available for petting. But if my hands move
too quickly, off she jumps, to return almost immediately, but poised to jump again. I am then expected to
soothe and caress her: first her shoulders, then her legs,
next her belly and finally her head—all are gently and
firmly stroked. Her eyes close as if in a trance. Her head
rests on my chest. There is communion.

Intelligence

Owners of animals derive no small degree of satisfac-
tion from alleging the extraordinary intelligence of
their wards and companions. And, naturally, owners of
wolf hybrids would like to have authoritative support
for their claim that the intelligence of the wolf and
wolf hybrid is superior to that of *Canis familiaris* or
Felis catus, for example. However, no set of tests can
overcome the obstacles inherent in the diverse goals,
objectives and equipment by which the intelligence of
different species and subspecies are measured. How
does one compare the intelligence of animals required
to solve different arrays of problems and provided with
different physical capabilities?

Let me illustrate. My house is never for long catless
and so, when old Stash passed peacefully on, I acquired
a furry, four-legged, female feline flasher of a Bluepoint
Siamese, whose given name was "Puffy." Now, old
Stash had become too arthritic to be much of a hunter
and my new house had been quickly infested with
what, in my former life as an economics professor, I
would have characterized as an infinitely elastic supply
of mice.

Wolves love winter snows.

Puffy, on the other hand, consistently snags two or three of the critters every night, shamelessly using my bedroom as a sort of Roman Coliseum. The thuds, squeaks, skitters, pounces and other goings–on are hardly conducive to rest. And so, in the first instance, an attempt was made to banish "P" to the rest of the house behind a closed door.

Sometime during the darkest hours of that first night, I became dully aware of being somehow suspended in space. My whole body was vibrating, and the center of that energy was on top of my chest. I opened my eyes and stared directly into those blue cat eyes of "P," who was smiling her cat smile and purring her heart out. Had she contrived to open the door? But the door was closed.

In the morning, I investigated and followed "P's" night path. The trail began in the kitchen. She had first

Chamaco in profile. His scars result from dominance battles.

climbed on a wastebin, then reached out and snagged the top of a drawer with her claws. She then pulled the drawer open and climbed in. She then proceeded into the space provided by the open drawer, gaining access to a hollow below the cabinets which led to the bedroom closet. The closet doors now presented a last obstacle.

Now "P" is about eight inches high at the withers and the doors are 80 inches high, a ratio of about one to ten. To appreciate her dilemma, say that you, 5'6" in height, have been set the problem of opening a door more than 55 feet tall and correspondingly heavy.... Somehow, in a fashion still not ascertained, "P" managed to open the monster from the inside. And this she must have accomplished fairly noiselessly, not waking me until she broke the silence with a purr.

My wolves, too, are now and again banished from the bedroom. Since, unlike "P," they cannot open the door or contrive entry by an alternate passage, they resign themselves to exile. Does that indicate a lower order of intelligence than that of a cat? Of course not, for while their objectives might be similar, their equipment differs. Wolves lack the sharp, retractable claws of *Felis catus,* and so have greater difficulty in grabbing and pulling with their paws. And even if it were easy for them to open cabinet drawers, they are too large to pass through. Attempting to compare the intelligence of wolves and cats is a futile exercise.

In some respects, the faculties of wolves are clearly superior to those of humans. Wolves, like dogs, can hear sounds long before we do. Smells are more readily identified by canids than by humans. These highly developed senses supply them with considerable data unavailable to humankind.

The problem-solving abilities of animals are tested in laboratories with the aid of mazes, bells and buzzers, food rewards and shock punishments. But what seems relevant to man may be of limited interest to an animal. For instance, scientists' attempts to hold dialogues with dolphins are only moderately sucessful, because dolphins seem to become bored with our limited human capacity to learn *their* language. Experiments with wolves and dogs that offer food rewards indicate that dogs, accustomed culturally and genetically to being provided for by humans, are slower in learning than wolves. Observation of my animals shows that the higher the percentage of wolf in the

Mariah! watching a rival.

mix, the more quickly will they figure out how to trip
the food hopper when they are hungry. In other words,
because wolves in the wild must fend for themselves,
they seem to have a greater problem–solving capacity
than do dogs when food is the reward.

On one occasion I observed some coyote behavior
that illustrates the wild canids' ability to use reason to
develop tactics to protect their interests. One fine afternoon, I was bulldozing a road down a mountainside in
Arizona. My dog was fussing about near the machine
when a large coyote approached and barked at her
aggressively. The coyote apparently did not see that a
human was attached to the bulldozer, and concen-
trated his attention on the dog. As I watched, his pur-

pose became evident. While he barked to distract the dog, his mate safely made her way up an arroyo behind him. After she had cleared the area, he backed away and followed her.

As an aside to this story, I should note that wolves and coyotes, being at least to some degree competitors, do not associate with each other. My wolves have never attacked coyotes but, in the few encounters I have witnessed, they quietly moved the coyotes off. The coyote will trot slowly ahead, followed by several wolves, until some invisible (to me) boundary is reached, and then the wolves retreat. In the interests of species survival, it would seem that wolves prefer not to engage in mortal combat when this is avoidable. This being so, it certainly is further evidence of their intelligence.

These large animals like to cuddle.

2

SELECTING A WOLF
HYBRID

Because they are protected from the substantial hazards of living free, wolf hybrids have a lifespan approximating that of *Canis familiaris*, usually approximately from a dozen to fifteen years. Since a wolf hybrid cub is likely to grow to maturity and live with its human companion for many years, a careful choice must be made. The setting in which the little fellow is brought into the world and the experiences of his early days will have considerable bearing on his ability to adjust, and on his physical and emotional health.

The mother wolf hybrid's role is very important. If she does not have a personality that appeals to you, there is a strong possibility that the cubs will not either.

Accordingly, never buy sight unseen, and always visit the mother and, if possible, the father, grandparents, aunts and uncles! I suppose that I learn slowly for, not once, but twice, I bought an animal sight unseen. One of them had not been adequately socialized and had

spent her days tied to a chain. She was unable to overcome that trauma, and never learned to relax or to act
responsibly in contact with other animals.

As the little cubs start to explore the world around
them, the older pack members begin to play important
roles in their lives. In the wild, uncles, aunts and cousins will have been feeding the nursing mother, but in
this instance they begin to take direct responsibility for
the cubs themselves. Frequently they groom and play
with the little ones. At about four weeks of age, the
cubs are given some easy lessons in submission. An
aunt or uncle will roll them over quite forcefully and
hold them on their backs until they relax and begin to
learn about the legitimacy of authority. This is a very
important step in the cub's progression into pack membership, and is somewhat akin to the sometime
accepted notion that children should respect their
elders. If the new owner of a wolf hybrid cub fully
understands that its acceptance of benignly but firmly
asserted authority is essential to the successful functioning of the pack, problems of training and integration into a new family (pack) will be minimized.

For this reason, I do not recommend taking a cub to a
new home before it is six weeks of age. Later is better
yet, but not always feasible if the breeder has good animals and many buyers waiting in line. The buyer
should observe, in addition to the mother, other adults
and subadults who are in training roles to the cub,
especially its father, whose behavior is imprinted both
through the gene pool and in his teaching role. Wolf
hybrid fathers are not always indulgent parents and
often get a little testy with their cubs. On the other
hand, aunts, uncles and cousins obviously greatly
enjoy playing with the cubs, and the best and most

willing teachers are subadults between one and two years of age.

When you first meet the cubs at the breeder's, naturally you will want to pick them up and get to know them. This is, of course, desirable, and the breeder should have been handling the young animals sufficiently to prepare them for this. They should be lifted and held comfortably in an upright position, not cradled on their backs. Since they tend to pick up an animal under the armpits, small children should not be allowed to hold them. If the cub is uncomfortable, it may struggle and fall.

Often people wiggle their fingers in front of a cub's face. This will generally make the cub nervous and cause him to back away. Never, never make a grabbing lunge at a cub. This will provoke fear and, perhaps, biting. I have had to spend weeks with cubs who have had this kind of careless treatment, trying to overcome their fright and get them used again to being handled.

Above all, be quiet and calm with the animal. Make no sudden movements or loud noises. Learn from the wolves' needs, how to be tactful and patient with them.

Sometimes I am asked how the mother hybrids feel when their cubs are swept away in the arms of loving, but apprehensive, strangers. Generally they *seem* quite unconcerned and return to their usual pursuits. Of my wolves, only one, Mariah!, a beautiful high-percentage lady, has shown any discernable reaction. I have seen her stretch up on her hind legs, whimpering, to sniff the wide-eyed little ball of fat. Perhaps the lack of specific attachment has a function in the wild, where infant mortality is high. There, the pack must go about its business in the face of loss. Grief may be there, but it also is probably short-lived.

For the human breeder or owner, the separation is harder, especially if the cub is the last of the litter. When the numbers have dwindled, more and more attention is focused on the few remaining. They are held and cuddled more, and their evolving personalities are savored. The longer an animal is with one, the more difficult the farewell, at least for the human. I try to encourage new owners to bring the cubs back to see their parents at my ranch, at least until the little guys are about six months old. The cubs and parents enjoy the visits and the owners and I can talk over cub development. But clearly my motives are not *entirely* unselfish.

Young cubs have a great deal of energy, vitality and curiosity, and are generally mischievous. Until they settle into lofty maturity, about two years of age, anything they can get their teeth around is fair game. Heavy rubber tanks full of water migrate all over the pens. Plastic dishes are nosed and skillfully batted around as though they were soccer balls. (But plastic can be deadly. Chamaco's mother died from ingesting Saranwrap that had encased some meat she stole.) A water hose carelessly left poking through the fence will be dragged to the other side and shaken to death. In this and several other respects, I find that wolf hybrids are more like cats than like dogs. If mice are so unfortunate as to enter the pens, they will be pounced on, played with, set down and watched, thrown into the air, chewed on, allowed to run off, and pounced on again, until they are nothing but a soggy mess.

Wolf hybrids like body contact and will rub against a favored person just as cats do. In hunting, they will sometimes dash after potential prey with wild abandon; and, at other times, proceed warily, stalking like mountain lions. Their games often involve ambush and quick pounces that roll their litter mates in the dirt. Wild, mad chases around the pens, over boulders—and people—and through the trees are enthusiastically pursued until all the participants are tuckered out.

Another appealing aspect of their nature is the wolf hybrid's strong need to give nuturance and to demonstrate affection. If you do not like to be hugged and kissed, choose another pet companion!

What other factors should be considered in the choice of an animal?

People who have previously owned wolf hybrids will often look for an animal that seems to promise a replication of their earlier experiences. This is an understandable desire, but not a realistic once. Within the general framework of wolfish behavior, each individual animal has a distinct personality. Purchase another wolf hybrid with the sure expectation that it will provide you with new experiences.

The percentage of wolf in an individual is a factor that many prospective buyers consider important. In general, but not always, the higher percentage animals will be more wolf-like in appearance, less tractable than dogs, and more wary and furtive. They also will be more expensive.

Knowledge and experience are cumulative. A person who buys a high percentage wolf hybrid, and who has not been involved with these animals previously, may not initially be able to provide the kind of care and handling that will enhance the best characteristics of the animal. The wolf hybrid's communication signals may not be understood. Irreversible mistakes may be made.

Many of these signals are complex and subtle. Although Chapters 3 and 4 offer some elucidation of this matter, individual and experiential variations preclude definitive statements. In order to read its humor and moods, there is no substitute for knowing an animal: when it may be bluffing or feigning aggression, when it will or will not respond to a command, and when not to push one's authority, to give a few examples. Only by intimate experience does one learn what situations require patience, what requires forgiving, when to bribe, when and how to chastise. This knowledge evolves from a sensitive process of give and take that cannot be codified into rules. Nor can the evolution of love and mutual respect between wolf and owner be hurried.

It is wise—very wise—to begin one's journey with wolf hybrids with low percentage (less than 75%) animals, and to learn from this experience before going up the scale. This is not to imply that high percentage animals are dangerous, but to emphasize that they are culturally different from dogs. If this differentiation is not recognized and respected, a rewarding interaction will never be fully achieved.

I believe that many buyers of wolf hybrids are motivated by a sense of support for and kinship with the wild wolf, and other wild creatures whose lives we cannot share, but only observe. The wolf hybrid, like the domestic cat, is a cultural mediator—one who is able to be reasonably comfortable in two cultures or two worlds—the domestic and the wild. This is what makes them fascinating.

What do wolves look like? Wolves, like humans, show great individual variation. In a given litter, there will be differences in the color pattern of the pelage (coat or fur), the color and shape of the eyes, and in overall size, physiognomy and conformation. Such variations facilitate the survival of the species.

Wolves mate for life and are very affectionate toward each other.

The most commonly held image of the wolf pictures him as long-bodied, gaunt and ragged, with skinny, splayed-out legs and big feet, and, more often than not, wearing a cruel expression. This is one possibility (except for the expression), but examination of many wolves reveals countless other possibilities. In Lawrence's *In Praise of Wolves*, there are several photographs of Tundra and Taiga. Tundra is all black with round, rather soft eyes. Taiga is gray, white and black, and her eyes are slanted and almond shaped. Tundra and Taiga are brother and sister. Neither exhibit the lanky legs and big feet referred to above. Those are more likely to be found among the tundra wolves who live among ice and snow, where such features are more adaptive.

With so much variation in physical appearance, it is impossible, and inadvisable, to set rigid standards for desirable features. However, the following elements might be used as a rough guide:

1. Body long and narrow.
2. Chest narrow.
3. Long legs with large feet.
4. Front legs slightly splayed when standing.
5. Small ears set wide apart.
6. Long, narrow muzzle.
7. Yellow or clear hazel eyes.
8. Tail bushy and flaccid at rest. Straight out (not curled over back) when in motion.
9. Black spot on top of tail, one-third of way from body.
10. Black tip at end of tail.
11. Flowing motion at slow lope.
12. Head held low at slow, steady trot.
13. Pronounced ruffs between cheeks and ears, and in front of and behind shoulders.

Except for the individuals that are all black or all white, gray tends to predominate. But wolves are likely to show black, gray and white, too, as well as rust color behind the ears and on the shoulders and legs. White, blending into gray, will show on the underside and muzzle. The gray is often the result of an admixture of black and white hairs. The colors typically are blended and very clear demarcation between black and white facial areas, such as one might see on a Siberian Husky, is not often found.

In winter, the wolf will have a thick undercoat that provides warmth and protection, and the guard hairs, especially on the ruffs, will thicken and lengthen. The coat contains a lanolin-like substance that provides waterproofing: if you rub your hand through the coat of a wolf or wolf hybrid, the skin will be pleasantly softened. The coats will shed in the spring and fall, so be prepared to gather bushels of the stuff to give to your local weaver. The fur spins easily into fine, strong threads, and sweaters made from it are reported to be exceptionally warm.

The cub that you buy will not likely show the color patterns of the older companion whose life you will share. Generally, the animals darken and show more complex patterns with age. My animals' winter coats tend to be darker than those of the summer. In more northerly and snowy areas, this pattern maybe reversed in the interests of camouflage and temperature control.

Size

When I ask other owners how much their wolves weigh, the answer is frequently "140 pounds." I cannot help wondering about this. I have some difficulty picking up a wolf of 90 pounds in order to weigh him, let alone others, such as Sitka, who weighs 112. Usually females weigh between 60 and 80 pounds, and males between 85 and 100. I have no doubt that some reach 140 pounds. But how does one verify that? A table in Mech's *The Wolf* tabulates wolf weights in North America and the Soviet Union. The largest animals out of a sample of 380 males and females weighed 133 pounds.* In the early 1970s, I interviewed a cowboy on the Arizona Strip who, at that time, was just a few weeks short of his 99th birthday. He reported that he had killed the last wolf in that country back about 1930. "Roped him off'n horseback," he said. And he (the wolf) weighed over 400 pounds. Yup! Shore thang!

While I do not like to see wolf hybrids on the downside of 60 pounds, a 90–pound animal is quite substantial—big enough to hug, but not too big to lift if necessary. Don't look for great size in your wolf companion. Other things are more important.

I am sometimes asked if wolves make good guard animals. In the usual sense, I think not. The wolf is a cautious, highly intelligent animal. These two characteristics associated with survival help the wolf to steer clear of scrapes unless they are unavoidable, or the odds are greatly in his favor and the prospect is irresistible. A pure wolf also is very suspicious of humans. He mistrusts and shuns them, with good reason, and therefore makes a poor watch animal.

One of the reasons that we hybridize wolves with dogs is to overcome this fear of man. The hybrid, therefore, may be more amenable to attack or protection training, but specific breeds of dogs are preferable for

*Mech, *op. cit.*, p. 12.

this purpose. Low percentage (i.e. 25 percent) wolf German Shepherds, similar in appearance to pure Shepherds, are sometimes bred and successfully trained for protection work. The higher percentage hybrids, 50 percent or more, are less suitable as guard animals, even though their appearance may be intimidating.

Nevertheless, animals without any training often seem to have acute powers of discrimination. For example, Chucho, a young male, was snoozing by the living-room fire in Santa Fe when he suddenly awoke in a state of agitation. After he was let outside, Chucho immediately dashed after an intruder who was hiding behind a car in the driveway. His owner restrained Chucho, and the intruder left, never to return.

The cubs that leave my ranch go to homes where they will be companions to people who delight in their positive, loving nature. I will not knowingly sell an animal to be used for guard or protection purposes. My wolves have intimidated undesirables and warned me of rattlesnakes, without specific training or command. In spite of their somewhat fierce appearance, many people are not frightened by them. When I lived in a small village south of Santa Fe, New Mexico, and my hybrids sometimes escaped, people, often strangers to me, would bring them back. Actually, because of their social nature, they delight in being visited and compete for the attention of guests.

Since owners and cubs are going to share space for many years, the choice needs to be carefully made. The buyer needs to appraise the cub's parents, the breeder, and the situation into which the cub has been born. The gene pool which determines the physical and psychological attributes of the cub goes back several generations, but, as has been said, the appearance and attitudes of the mother and father are highly significant in providing some clues as to how the cub will develop. If there is something about the parents that makes you uncomfortable or wary, check further.

I say *some* clues, since cubs go through changes in color and personality as they develop. This is not a case of "what you see is what you get." In my experience, colors will tend to darken with age, the later conformation will be quite different, and personalities will evolve. Some cubs are quite shy when little, but in a nurturing environment their personalities will blossom. Do not be put off by cubs that run away from you or hide. This is usually a short-lived phase.
Wolves, as they mature, go through a number of changes, both physiologically and behaviorally. For instance, the muzzle is initially quite short but lengthens with time. Neotony refers to the retention by the adult of juvenile characteristics. The Pekinese and the Bulldog exemplify severe neotonic arrest in domestic dogs. Wolf cubs transit through a heel-nipping phase that remains fixed in the Blue Heeler, for instance. In other words, domestic dogs are specialized adaptations of phases of the wolf's evolution from cub to adult. It is therefore quite proper to speak of the dog as descending from the wolf.

How can the buyer appraise the breeder? In this case, "what you see *is* what you get." Observe how the breeder relates to the animals and, better still, how the animals relate to him. Is there affection and respect between them? Does the breeder exert firm but gentle discipline? Are the pens spacious and clean? Are the animals in good spirits and accepting of people? Is the breeder professional and businesslike? Are your questions satisfactorily answered?

Some breeders have no qualms about selling higher percentage wolf hybrids to people who have no prior experience with the animals. Others will knowingly sell to people who cannot provide the animals with the facilities and companionship that they need. Sellers have the serious responsibility, in the best interests of both the buyers and the animals, to carefully match client and cub, and not to sell to people who cannot provide for all the wolves' important needs.

Be wary of buying an animal that has been chained. This practice can be very destructive and bring out bad qualities. Because wolves are so social, they should be allowed to share pens, although, since individuals sometimes develop strong animosities, separation is required now and again.

The cub should have had his first inoculations at six weeks of age. If the shots are given the day that they leave, the cub is likely to be upset and may not travel well. Even so, the first car ride may be traumatic, so it is wise to be prepared with newspapers and old towels.

The Wolf Hybrid Cub at Home

From the earliest possible time, the cub should have been handled by a number of people. This will aid in the transition to new surroundings. Wolf hybrids are unhappy in solitude. The company of people and dogs or cats promotes their healthy emotional development. Now and again I sell my cubs to a person who lives alone and who has no other pets, but in that case, usually it will be a person who works at home, or can take the cub on visits to other places. In one such instance the owner operated a health club where Chaco would lie quietly beneath a desk and not bother the patrons. Only when given permission would he venture out to be petted by a patron or employee.

How a wolf hybrid will get along with a dog usually will depend upon the dog. If an older dog accepts a cub, all will be well, unless it has bad habits that the cub will emulate. If the dog is threatened by the new addition, the cub will be rebuffed in its efforts to make friends. This is an unstable situation that the cub may accept for the time being, but might later challenge when it feels it can dominate the dog. Dogs often do not understand the complex language of wolves and may know nothing of the hierarchy of authority that a wolf, or wolf hybrid, considers natural. The cub will want to know where he fits within the new people–and–animal structure. His initial approach to a dog usually will be an offer of submission, manifested by mouth licking, furious tail wagging, squirming and rolling over. The dog may not understand these gestures and also may be bewildered by the cub's tremendous energy. For its part, the cub may be confused by the dog's response or lack thereof. In his need for hierarchy, it is likely that he will attempt to dominate the resident domestic animals, stealing their food and generally pushing them around. Of course, this will not necessarily happen, especially if the cub meets with a good reception. There may be harmony and joy in the canine society. But the cub does fit better into a structured situation where there is good leadership and discipline and each animal knows its place.

Cats and wolf hybrids can get along famously. Indeed, one of the things that impressed me about the first wolf hybrid that came into my life was his affection and loyalty towards the four cats of the housefold. One cannot count on such happy outcomes, however, and the introduction of these two species to each other should be conducted with care and tact. Wolf hybrid cubs constantly test new situations. Their rough and tumble way with other cubs will be quite unacceptable to a cat. But because the young cub is, for awhile, of the same size order as a cat, the cub's natural inclination is to test and play with the cat as he would with other cubs. Usually, a cat will effectively cut short that kind of nonsense by delivering a swat on the nose. If a cub tries to provoke a cat into a chase, the cat is at a tactical disadvantage. If it then does not use its natural defenses to protect itself, the owner should immediately slap the cub, or hold it securely and speak to it firmly, letting it know that roughness will not be tolerated. My cats and wolf hybrids have become firm friends and engage in much nuzzling and purring. It is heartwarming to see a cat curled up against the grown canid, content, warm and safe.

Cats seem to know which hybrids can be trusted and which cannot. They can instantaneously read the hybrids' intentions, and read it correctly. When a hybrid that is potentially menacing, even if only in its youthful boisterousness, enters the room, cats will disappear like a slate swept clean. When other wolves, even those newly met, project qualities that are non-threatening, cats will be ready to tease and play—or just confidently go back to sleep.

Wolves and wolf hybrids can become very agitated by the movement of horses, which can represent for them playmates or prey. Buffalo wolves bring down prey by grabbing the victim's muzzle and stubbornly holding on. When Chaco first met my horses, he jumped for the nose, following instinct. But instead of grabbing a bite, he deflected his thrust and licked the horse's nostril. Baby Dan was a mite startled by this at first, but grew to accept this lupine affection.

Since wolves and wolf hybrids love young things,

they tend to accept children and are adored by them in return. However, it is important for children and adults to understand the difference between teasing and playing. Human children or adults may engage in play with them for hours on end, and still will tire before the wolf hybrids do. But if the human teases, the wolf hybrid will grow angry and snap. Any injury that results will not be the fault of the canid. The wolf hybrid may for a short while tolerate being used as a drum, but he will not accept it for long. If the animal has no way of escape, it will feel that it has to defend itself. If a child does not have an innate sense of discipline, this lack will transfer to the cub. Parents should reflect on the situation in their household before making a commitment to an animal of this kind. Occasional reports in the press of attacks by wolf hybrids and pet wolves get considerable attention, because of the traditionally negative image of the wolf. Whether the pet wolf or wolf hybrid is more dangerous than any given breed of dog is hard to establish because of insufficient data. However, because of the acute sensitivity of wolves and wolf hybrids, there are protective measures that can be taken. Animals that are constantly chained, especially those that receive no ameliorating human care, are likely to become frustrated, anxious and angry. If such an animal is then taunted, or perhaps stoned, by a child or children, one has a prescription for tragedy. A child, cat or dog that then strays within range of the wolf's or wolf hybrid's extended chain is likely to be attacked. When only the attack and not the circumstances that provoked it are then publicized, ordinances enforcing unreasonable restrictions and prohibitions can result. Some characteristic behavior of children, such as rapid, erratic movements, squealing, tumbling and rolling, resemble that of wounded prey, exciting primitive instincts in animals. For this reason, children should be monitored carefully when at play with wolf hybrids until their parents are confident that they and the hybrids can develop a safe modus operandi. Over the years I have become increasingly concerned about the hazards that face animals that wander without supervision. Unless I am hiking or running with them, my hybrids are either in their pens or in the house. I keep them from the temptation to chase game or cattle or to slaughter chickens, and protect them from the danger of getting stolen or run over. By the same token, the cats of my household never go outside to be exposed to hazards, or, for that matter, to deplete bird populations. The cats, too, seem reasonably content with their protected status.

3

TRAINING THE WOLF HYBRID

It is said that wolves are not readily trainable. To this I cannot speak, since I have had little experience with wolves. Wolf hybrids, however, are quite trainable, provided that the process is undertaken with care and begun early enough.

Because it is not necessary, my own animals do not receive formal, systematic training. Wolves in the wild learn through the discipline of the pack, and this is the framework that I am able to utilize with the hybrids.

The young cubs get their first lessons at about four weeks. Mother is getting sore from their sharp little teeth and snaps at them when her teats begin to hurt. Other younger, mature, but unrelated animals, also in the pen, play with them and assist in their training. The first and most important lesson is in submission. An adult will grab the cub by a foreleg and roll it over on its back. It will be held there until it relaxes and stops making noises of protest. The cubs thus learn about benign authority and that the path to greatest gain is the one of least resistance.

As much as possible, I let the older hybrids undertake the teaching. Wolves (and dogs and cats) learn a great deal from mature models. I used Chamaco, for instance, a level-headed male of four years of age, to test, train and lead Mariah!, an enormously intelligent, high-percentage hybrid. Mariah! adored Chamaco and respected him. She saw Chamaco respond instantly when called by name and she very quickly learned hers and would whip around on hearing it. On our first walks, Mariah! followed like a shadow at my heels, stopping when I stopped, sitting when I sat, looking where I looked. As she learned the routine and developed confidence in herself, she also began to observe Chamaco. Only the three of us would tramp the hills at first, but others joined later. As we roamed, the wolf hybrids coursed ahead rather like scouts, and ever so silently I would plod behind. Without being called, they checked back on me from time to time. Atsay is a long-legged hybrid of tundra wolf extraction who charges back at full speed and comes to a sliding stop, scattering sand in my face. This is something that Mariah! decided she had to try too, but her young legs were not fully developed and she lacked the style of Atsay.

Proceeding in this way, the learning is a relaxed, gradual process, without anxiety. Benign authority stands ready if called upon. There are strong words if there is even a hint of challenge or questioning of this authority. If a spank is necessary it is immediate and brief. Remember—tact and patience. Add to these firmness, fairness and restraint, and love.

This recommendation is based upon the critical assumption that the cub's parents and pack mates are well adjusted and thoroughly socialized animals. If such is not the case, and other evidence indicates that the animal is one that would fit into a new home, an early transfer is preferable.

In the wild, the highly dependent cubs are cared for by all members of the pack and find the world is a friendly place. Not so after they leave the den. Taiga and tundra are full of such hazards as porcupines and bears. Survival requires caution. In some way, either through genetic programming or through messages from the mother wolf, the cubs learn this caution and are wary of strangers. A wild cub cannot readily transfer bonding and allegiance to a human once it has left the den. For that reason, some breeders believe that cubs should go to new homes as early as eight days of age, and never more than 16. In such cases, the new owner will have to be prepared to bottle feed and, consequently, there is some risk of disease for the little fellow, since he is deprived of the immunity he would normally receive from the mother's milk.

The early training of a wolf or wolf hybrid, whether received in the context of the pack family or the human family, becomes deeply imprinted. Patterns of behavior seem to be generalized into a code that extends beyond the immediate and defined lesson.

I saw a rather graphic example of this which may suggest that wolf hybrids have a sense of right and wrong. One morning when I went out to feed them, the pack was *extremely* quiet. I was not mobbed as usual, and there was no horseplay, no hugging, no licking. I thought nothing of it until I went inside the horse trailer where the feed was stored and found the lid off a bin and a *large* amount of food gone—obviously into six plump stomachs. I looked out of the trailer. There was a deathly silence and no sign of the thieves except for an ill-concealed tail sticking out from beneath

some logs. Although I was bursting with repressed
laughter, I could not possibly disappoint the mis-
creants. So I let out a bellow of rage, banged some cans
around, and stalked out of the pen. Later, all was for-
given but not forgotten, and they seemed relieved that
their only punishment was the withholding of their
usual breakfast—which, obviously, they hardly
needed.

If animals have some sense of permissible and imper-
missible behavior, it follows that they should be justly
treated. They are likely to resent arbitrary punishment.
But if some punishment were not meted out for misbe-
havior, it is to be expected that they would lose respect
for the person in authority.

Should there be some truth in these speculations,
the owner must not hesitate to punish and reward.
Punishment should be firm but fair, immediate and
short lived. Incarceration for a "crime" extends too
long to be functional; indeed it can breed resentment.
A sharp slap and a verbal tongue lashing are more effective: "no" or "stay" are often sufficient. If the wolf
hybrid still does not heed, or if the transgression is serious, the ultimate punishment is to grab the animal,
throw him on his back, hold him by the shoulders
above the forelegs, and shake him, while scolding him
and looking sternly into his eyes. If his tail curves up
over the groin and he pees on himself, the message has
been received and understood.

As a disciplinary device, the shoulder roll should
hardly ever be needed. However, I use it as part of a
game. All my animals are rolled like this occasionally,
while being held gently and firmly. This is accompanied by stroking and playful shaking in a non-
threatening way. If one uses this approach, the wolf

hybrid is less likely to challenge the disciplinary shoulder roll when it is needed.

The monks of New Skete refer to the shoulder roll as the *alpha*-wolf roll-over. This is the method they recommend: "Don't casually guide the dog over as if you were going to groom it or play with it. Shove the dog onto its back with vigor. At this point, most dogs will go into the classic submissive posture of all canids."*

My approach is slightly different. If the hybrids have learned the shoulder roll as cubs, they understand the nuances of its significance. When the mature animals first subject them to it they squeal mightily, but soon learn that they will not be hurt if they relax and do not resist. If the owner emulates the methods of the older wolves, he will develop the necessary skill and confidence, and the cub will be less likely to resist. By varying the strength and roughness of his throwing, by intonation of his voice and modulation of facial expressions, the owner can convey to the wolf his intent, whether of play or discipline, and, if the latter, the degree of severity involved.

Punishment should be rarely needed. Verbal approval or disapproval usually are sufficient to keep order.

Most important of all, both for discipline and harmony, is the establishment of a strong bond between owner and wolf hybrid. Mere feeding is insufficient to achieve this, even though animals generally look favorably upon those who provide for them. Bonding comes from physical contact—hugging, stroking and caressing. Each of my animals gets a kind of massage

*The Monks of New Skete, *How to be Your Dog's Best Friend: A Training Manual for Dog Owners,* Little, Brown & Co., Boston-Toronto, 1978.

once or twice a day. Along the back, chest and legs, I work with hands and fingers. Watch their eyes close contentedly as you work. They will rub their heads and bodies against yours in sharing and communion.

Remember that wolves, as a group, are animals with strong needs to give and receive nurturing and affection, as amply demonstrated by their mutual nuzzling, licking and mouthing. When they interact with humans, the manifestations are somewhat different. Like felines, wolf hybrids try to rub their bodies against a person, but sometimes get unbalanced and fall if the person shifts position. Face licking, especially if one has a moustache, is enthusiastic and persistent. Newcomers are often unnerved when my wolves place huge paws on their shoulders, the better to look into their startled eyes. Chicha, a friendly female, has a pointed nose noted for its unerring accuracy when aimed at the delicate interstices of human anatomy. Some hybrids are lap sitters who quietly and coyly insinuate themselves upon a person who is comfortably seated. If a person is not demonstrative and rebuffs the animal's affectionate overtures, he will obstruct the development of an important aspect of the hybrid's nature, and limit the potential intensity of the relationship.

Wolf hybrids are not wild, as the term is generally understood, even though they seem to have the capability to cross the interface between wild and tame, as does the domestic cat. They are sensuous and delight, for example, in being groomed, or rolling in horse guano, or giving voice to their bell-like howl. Their *play* is often wild, crazy and free, especially on being let out of their pens. Their sexual flirtation is playful but becomes quite businesslike as they proceed to tie.

A depth of intensity is expressed when they look

directly into a person's eyes, or when their mournful cry wells up from deep inside them. Their other-directedness is marked, contrasting with, for example, some of the self-centered toy canines that constantly yap demands for attention, giving little in return.

As mentioned previously, the wild wolf pack, while structured and hierarchical, is not a static organization. It can change with variations in the environment and the number and types of prey. Wolves die and cubs are born. Survival calls for adaptation to new circumstances. And so leadership and intra-pack ranking are subject to alteration. Lower ranking wolves will probe and test the structure, and new leaders may emerge.

The same will be true of a pack of wolf hybrids. An injured *alpha* male may lose his dominant position to a junior, perhaps his son. When Chaco fell out of a pickup truck he broke a hind leg and, in spite of the repair with two steel pins, never returned to full mobility. Chamaco, his good-natured son, challenged Chaco and assumed the dominant position in an uneasy alliance never quite accepted by Chaco.

The breeding season is a time of tensions within the pack and also for the breeder of wolf hybrids. Not only do the males have an understandable interest in the females in *estrus*, but the females become very competitive, as well. This is a time when an established order of wolves can be upset. The female who is mating becomes aggressive and, if her status was subordinate previously, this may now be changed. Females who had once gotten along famously become permanent enemies. When they encounter each other, hackles are raised, lips curl, growls emanate from below, and pushing and shoving ensues. The new *alpha* may attack and knock the other down, very much to her surprise. The males then become agitated and a battle starts among them. Old indignities are remembered and scores are settled. When the dust settles, a new structure may have evolved. Pity the poor breeder whose wolf hybrid pack is battling, amid flowing blood, loud screams and fearsome growls. How does he stop the slaughter?

I have tried dousing the combatants with water, thumping on them with anything handy, and even resorted to bad words. No luck. If only two are fighting and another person is there, ready, willing and able, tails can be grabbed and the wolves pulled apart— slowly, firmly and carefully. The best solution is, of course, prevention: keep antagonists separated. I also have used radio training collars with great effect. These collars transmit a brief electric shock when a button on a transmitter is pressed. They get the animal's attention if used correctly.

Careful management may avert these situations, but a human *alpha*, even if never before threatened or challenged, should not become complacent. A challenge is rare. Indeed, I have never experienced anything approaching a threat from any of my animals. You may, however, be tested, just to find out if you really mean what you say. And if a person fears his or her animals, this will be perceived, and the ability to control will be compromised.

While the cub is still younger than six months, the owner's goal will be to establish a harmonious communion with the little fellow. Treats—perhaps small pieces of beef fat—will help to stimulate a positive association with the owner. The cub should be picked up quietly and gently. It should be introduced to other animals—cats, horses, birds—and restrained from chasing them, but encouraged to friendly curiosity.

Short, smooth rides in a car, possibly ending with a treat such as an ice cream cone, are a good idea. If this is not done, a car ride can panic the cub into emitting from both ends.

Since most owners will keep their wolves inside much of the time, housebreaking becomes an important concern. Once should expect "accidents" at first and try not to strain the natural limits of the young wolf's storage capacity. In other words, let it outside at first at frequent, and then less frequent, intervals. Some lucky owners acquire an animal who cottons on immediately and they never have to clean up a mess. Other cubs take longer. One couple followed my instructions with their female cub, oh, so carefully. They were kind, patient, quiet, forbearing. But Chiska dumped deposit after deposit on their light-colored dining room rug. Patience has a limit, especially when it seems to bear no fruit. When yet another outrage occurred, Stan and Nancy finally exploded in righteous wrath. That did it. The transgressions ceased for good. Chiska had finally gotten the message. This only goes to prove how difficult it is to established general rules for the training of all wolves.

The wolf hybrid passes through adolescence from about six to 24 months of age and this can be a difficult transition. From a roly-poly cuddly cub it becomes, like a human teenager, often ornery and disobedient. One manifestation of this is a fear of entrapment. It may not be willing to approach a person because that person may grab its collar and do goodness knows what to it. Or it may not come when called, trotting off as though it had not heard a thing. When he returns with the family from a walk, the hybrid may suddenly take off again and not show up for an hour or so. Or else it

may not want to go into the pen at the owner's command. These are the times one sometimes wishes one
had never heard of a wolf hybrid. When the animal is
running madly over hill and dale there is not much
comfort in recalling the breeder's assurances that this
phase too shall pass.

There are no sure solutions to all the problems of
wolf hybrid juvenile delinquency. However, Pavolovian
approaches sometimes work. I keep no food or water
outside the compound, so my animals *must* return to
satisfy these basic needs. When I leave for a walk, the
compound gate is left open (I leave for a walk, *they*
leave for a run). When they come dashing back their
thirst leads them straight for the water trough. If they
are reluctant to enter the pen, I entice them in with
some toast or old bread. No pen, no food. But since
they *expect* to be fed at certain times and places, they
tend to behave in predictable and desirable ways.

Getting them to come to a call when they are running out in the woods can be managed in several ways.
One technique is to have young or recalcitrant animals
go out in the company of obedient, disciplined animals. Another is to play games with them, such as
hide-and-seek. You play at hiding and they will find
you with great delight. Another device is to pretend to
abandon them—maybe even driving off if they are not
at the parking area when you are ready to leave after a
hike. This can induce panic and may only need to be
used once for a particular animal.

The training manuals for dogs recommend the use of
a long training rope which is used to haul them in if
they fail to respond when called or to other commands.
With an older animal, I use a lunge line of the type
used for training horses. It is made of webbing, has a

snap to tie on to the collar or harness, and a loop that can be held. The lunge line is heavy enough to slow an animal down and can be easily grabbed when necessary. I sometimes use it with aggressive animals. The weight on the line is sufficiently distracting to curb some of their energy and the restraint puts the aggressor at a tactical disadvantage.

The techniques offered by most training manuals for dogs are usually effective with wolf hybrids, but may need to be adapted. In many cases the manuals are oriented to show ring performance, and present an almost militaristic view of owner and animal. Part of the delight of associating with a wolf hybrid lies in its contact with a wilder world. Your aim should be to allow the expression of that untamed spirit, but within the parameters of reasonable human requirements. This requires a subtle balance of sensitivities to two different worlds and is one of the reasons that owning wolf hybrids is not for everyone.

There is a very effective training device, the radio training collar, which costs about $200, and has many applications. It can be used, for example, in training dogs to come when called, in inhibiting barking, and in curbing aggression. It elicits an immediate response, that is quickly learned and strongly imbedded. From a distance of up to a quarter of a mile, one can administer an attention-getting charge when an animal is not responding to a command. Usually this need be done only once or twice to achieve the desired result.

Some persons may be offended by what seems the cruelty of this method, but the shock is instantaneous and sharp and will not do damage unless misused. Administering this brief shock, it seems to me, is preferable to having your animal crushed by a car or mangled in a fight.

Wolves can be very wary of the new and unexpected. As mentioned earlier, if I walk into the pens wearing a strange hat, some of the higher percentage animals will spook, running to the far fence and giving off alarm barks. They often react similarly to tall or bulky men and women. It has been hypothesized that wolves read in such people signs and mannerisms that say BEAR, the only natural enemy of the wolf. We should be sensitive to these fear-inducing possibilities if we wish to keep our animals calm.

Two litters of mine were born early one cold, stormy winter. The below-freezing temperatures, ice and snow seemed never ending. It was difficult to spend outdoor time handling the cubs and it was a period of stress for all. These litters proved extremely hard to socialize and, for this reason, I now try to avoid having litters that will be born from November through February. But there may be another explanation for the problem. Because of the cold I was always bundled in layers of garments when I entered the pens and moved with less than my usual catlike grace (ahem!). Could it be that this awkward, bulky figure that loomed at the entrance to the den each dawn and evening evoked the atavistic image BEAR for the young cubs?

What about the older wolf hybrid? How will this animal fit into new surroundings? That depends, of course, on the new surroundings and on how the animal has been treated previously. By six months of age, behavior patterns are well established. If these are positive, all will go well. If not, the process of retraining may take years. This is particularly true if the animal lacks discipline and will not heed the call to come. Hours of training, perhaps even professional training, may be necessary.

Since I wrote this chapter, Ernie Smith published

Warm Hearts and Cold Noses,* which offers perceptions and observations based on his many years as a dog
trainer. This is a sensitive and valuable book and deals
very effectively with some of the questions just discussed. As to Ernie's thoughts on the parallel development of wolves and dogs, one has to say that the jury is
still out and may well starve to death before it reaches a
verdict.

*Ernie Smith, *Warm Hearts and Cold Noses,* Sunstone Press, Santa Fe,
1987.

4

COMMUNICATION

 We human beings have come to rely almost exclusively on the spoken and written word to convey our thoughts and feelings. And how inadequate they are! A close association with wolves and wolf hybrids exposes us to other channels and, if we are open to it, can teach us about feelings that we have allowed to atrophy.

One aspect of the language of wolves is well known. The howling we associate with wolves is certainly used by them more frequently and eloquently than by dogs. Sharing your life with a pack of them, you come to appreciate that no two howls are the same. Each time they sing, a different chorus is intoned. Their delight is apparent as they discover new sounds, harmonies and counterpoints. Usually the howl is begun by one individual, the chorus master. He sets the tone and mood and the others ululate along, sometimes punctuating passages with yips and barks. The song drifts for awhile, then, as though cued by a baton, all the wolves stop at the same instant. The reason for this is not

Chica howling. Wolves' songs distinguish them from other canids and are extremely important in uniting the pack.

readily apparent. If I give a shout in mid-song, it can have the same effect. This causes me to speculate that the wolves stop singing in order to listen for a response, perhaps from the individual who initiated the chorus.

The human receptor can only guess at the import of the various wolf songs. One that I hear often has a very clear meaning, however. As I walk or drive away from the house and pens, leaving the pack behind, the chorus of complaint is unmistakable. "Owowow! The sonvabitch is abandoning us again!"

Remote, rumbling trains tell the pack that a diesel horn will soon sound at the crossing, and that, as well as church bells from the distant village, sets them off. The yipping and cachinnating of coyotes, who know that the wolf hybrids are confined and cannot run them off, are a certain source of agitation.

Some howls seem to arise from the very depth of wolf souls. These are night songs that begin with a low mournful solo several measures long. A second voice may join in counterpoint and then a third, fourth and more. It is hard to imagine a more profound expression of nature. Its mystery reaches down into the depths of the listener's being.

Occasionally one hears a solo song, without chorus. In my pack, Sitka usually is the soloist in a melody with variations, a melancholy cry of six or seven notes within an octave. After this first offering, he lowers his head, yawns, pauses reflectively and wails the same phrase again but with a slight difference, perhaps prolonging a note, using a glissando, or adding a note or two. There may be ten or more variations on the initial theme which is never exactly duplicated. It seems as if a thought process and experimentation are involved.

Of course, wolves and wolf hybrids can and do bark.

Fortunately, this is rare and purposeful. If a wolf hybrid barks, pay attention, for something is amiss—there is a rattlesnake in the pen, or a strange, unwelcome human. These are barks of warning or challenge. Other barks may express frustration, as when, for instance, a male wants to enter a pen and share the company of an attractive female.

Other vocalizations include growls, snarls, whines, whimpers, and something blending whine and howl that might be called mouthing. These sounds often are complemented with body language. The placement of legs, tail and head all convey signals and messages. A tail straight out behind, with head slightly lowered, front legs stiffened, eyes fixed on yours, accompanied by a low growl, constitutes a distinct warning. The animal is positioned to leap, one hopes not at the throat.

Body language is always significant. Forelegs can be used like arms to hug other wolves and favored persons. A licking tongue expresses friendliness and affection.

Wolf hybrid faces are quite mobile. Lips can be raised to show teeth. Rounded eyes may indicate alert curiosity. An *alpha* male, surrounded by sycophantic *betas*, will hold his head high, and his fixed expression brings to mind a Latin American *caudillo* strutting with his subordinates through some public function.

This analysis of wolf communication, as well as those by authors such as Mech and Zimen, among others, excellent though they are, are still inadequate. The communication is subtle and dynamic, and the printed page is a poor substitute for hearing and seeing. Often, there is too much going on for the mind to encompass, record and recapitulate it all. But in the immediate experience, watching and listening, often it is possible to interpret a whole spectrum of meanings:

this wolf is angry, that one is unsure of himself, the other is just moony-eyed lovestruck. Few owners have difficulty in understanding their animal's messages, even though the articulation of the array of signals may defy formulation.

But, as is the case with fellow humans so with wolves: the thoughts and feelings of another being can sometimes be opaque to us, reaching us as they do through the possibly distorting filters of our own emotions.

5

CARE AND FEEDING

Some owners and breeders, perhaps in an effort to simulate natural conditions, feed their animals nothing but raw meat. Not only is this expensive, but it may result in aggressive, competitive eating which contributes to tension and management problems. The manner in which the animals are fed also may have something to do with aggression and competition. If a leg of venison alone is hurled into a pen where there are several animals, this is asking for trouble. If feed dishes are widely separated and there is more than sufficient meat, little harm may occur.

Meat also may affect the animals' smell: their smell, not sense of smell. A friendly rancher once provided me with the residue of butchering—offal and some hooves. My, how the gang stunk. They were banned from house and vehicle for days. They just smelled offal.

A quality dry food and sufficient water are adequate to keep the animals in good condition and control their weight. Food hoppers (dispensers) that allow snacking will reduce competitive anxiety. My animals who have access to these feeders rarely gain excess weight. One who was overweight lost excess pounds when he did not have to compete at mealtimes.

Large bones may be given once a week, but make certain that there are more bones in the pen than there are wolf hybrids. Such bones are good for the teeth and keep the pack members happily occupied for some time. The bones will, of course, be buried and resurrected frequently.

Feeding should not be done perfunctorily. Unless you are strapped for time, use the dinner hour as a time for communication and demonstrations of affection. My animals insist on giving and receiving hugs and kisses, or having a free-for-all chase around the pen, *before* they eat. This reflects an important part of wolf protocol. When wolves come together after a separation, there usually is enthusiastic sniffing, licking, tailwagging and gesticulation. My entry into the pens, then, also is a time for the reaffirmation of bonds. The animals insist on licking my face and jostle each other for the chance. For my part, I hug them, rub legs and tummies, and affirm the joy and privilege of knowing them.

Wolf hybrids who spend a lot of time indoors may develop dry coats and skins, which a little fat or margarine will remedy. Nursing mothers will be drawn down considerably and need a fat or protein supplement. Raw eggs also may be in order for pregnant hybrids or nursing mothers. They love the eggs, which help to keep them in good condition.

Some wolf hybrids are notorious landscape artists and mining engineers and spend a lot of time digging holes and tunnels. When the pens are not well con-

Feeding should not be done in a perfunctory manner. It is an important opportunity for a daily bonding ceremony.

structed, the temptation to dig out and go exploring is irresistible. Several things can be done to prevent this. The most expensive is to build deep concrete footings below the fencing wire. Pressure-treated lumber is more cost effective and quicker to install. The wire that I have found to be both effective and easy to install has rectangular mesh about two by four inches and is of a gauge no less than 12½. Even this gauge could be severed by an aggressive animal or a large male interested in a female in season. Heavier gauges are available. Do not use stock fencing with larger holes, because cubs may scramble through something larger than two by four inches or, when animals are agitating each other near a fence, one may have its head pulled through and get hurt. A jealous female might try to pull another mother's cub through a fence and could possibly kill it.

Some owners bury wire mesh in the ground, extending it inward from the fence about eighteen inches. Others use a low voltage electric fence a foot above grade. Wolf hybrids can easily scale or jump a five- or six-foot fence, but a hot wire at the top of the fence line will stop them. This should be checked periodically for grounding. In some urban jurisdictions, electric fences may not be legal.

The smallest pens for two to four animals should be about 2500 square feet. Ideally, there should be trees and rocks to give the feeling of a natural environment. Each pen should have a "jungle gym" with an elevated platform from which the wolf hybrids can view their surroundings. The recommended area will afford sufficient space for them to chase each other and get adequate exercise, relieving the owner of a sometime burden. Wolves, and wolf hybrids, seem to have a higher metabolism than dogs and the freedom and opportunity to exercise are essential to their physical and mental well being.

Wolves and wolf hybrids have self-cleaning coats. A lanolin-like oil waterproofs them. If you rub your hands through the fur, the skin will feel wonderfully softened.

Wolf hybrids often sleep soundly in snow or driving rain. But this does not mean that shelter should not be provided. It is essential that they be able to get out of the hot summer sun or a hard rain. A simple shelter that keeps them comfortable can be made of bales of straw topped by a piece of plywood. But supplemental heat need not be provided, even for nursing mothers. If the living space is well constructed, the animals' body heat will provide sufficient warmth.

Breeders of hybrid wolves may disagree about the characteristics of their ideal animal. From the standpoint of health, this is desirable, ensuring against the hazards of insistence upon a rigid conformation and pattern of color. The hybrid gene pool of the total population is constantly refreshed as new wolves and dogs enter the breeding interchange, reducing the possibilities of physical deformities such as the hip dysplasia frequently found in German Shepherds. Better mental health is another favorable result of avoiding intensive inbreeding. It is wise to see several animals that have originated with your breeder, if possible, and discuss with the owners their experiences with and evaluations of them.

In general, wolf hybrids react similarly to dogs to medical treatment. However, as Dorothy Prendergast writes:

> A high percentage Wolf Hybrid may be much more sens-
> tive to medications than a dog of the same weight, and
> care should be taken that it does not receive overdoses of
> any medication.
>
> Dorothy Prendergast, *The Wolf Hybrid*, Rudelhaus Enter-
> prises, Gallup, NM, 1984, p. 52.

Any owner can practice the preventive medicine
necessary to keep his animals healthy, even to the
extent of giving vaccinations. Whatever you do, however, should be done in consultation with a veterinarian. When my cubs are six weeks of age I give them
their first set of shots against canine distemper, hepati-
tis, parainfluenza and parvovirus. With someone else
holding the cub, you can easily administer a sub-
cutaneous injection in the shoulder, with apparently
little discomfort to the cub.

However, the common multipurpose vaccines do not
always give full protection against the parvovirus. One
morning I found a ten-week-old cub lying stretched
out and listless. I rushed him to the vet, who diagnosed
parvo. Sicus barely pulled through after a week of
intensive care. He had received two sets of shots, one at
six weeks and the other just before the symptoms were
noted. Apparently, the standard vaccines will not
always overcome the natural immunity that cubs
receive from their mother and there was a lapse in the
protection between the first and second vaccinations.
My practice now is to immunize for parvo alone at six
weeks, using a vaccine that is said to override the
mother's natural immunity. I follow this with the full
set of shots, starting at eight weeks of age.

How Sicus contracted parvo remains a mystery. I dis-
courage visitors from bringing dogs to the property, but
the virus might have been carried in on someone's

shoes. Parvo is now reported among wild wolves. The coyotes that roam this area may have contracted it also.

One malady that is difficult to eradicate is the tapeworm. An infected mother can transmit the worms to her unborn babies and this can reduce their immunity to other infections. My animals are regularly dewormed, but transmission from the environment is difficult to prevent. Rabbits are hosts to these worms and this is reason enough not to allow your animals to hunt.

Rattlesnakes are another disagreeable hazard of desert living and they find their way into the pens now and again. The caution bark of wolves is very distinct. Once Mariah! warned me in this way of a rattlesnake in her pen. Just as I had the rattler fixed in the sights of my revolver and was squeezing the trigger, a cub ran between me and the snake. I held my fire and the snake did not strike, perhaps sensing the danger from me. After the rattler was dispatched, the wolves in the pen had a royal time flinging it around until it was nothing but pulp. I have yet to find a way to protect cubs from rattlesnakes, but, during the summer, I always have the .22 magnum revolver ready and loaded with birdshot.

Mention should be made of man-made hazards that can kill wolves and cubs. Soon after weaning her cubs, Chamaco's mother died from Saranwrap poisoning. She had eaten meat wrapped in plastic and could not eliminate it. Sometimes well-meaning people throw food and playthings into the pens, which should be checked frequently to avert the problems they can cause.

Wolf hybrids are large, vigorous animals and their mental and physical health will be endangered if they are confined in cramped, uncomfortable surroundings. Two or more should be kept together in a large pen, so that they can run and play together and, equally important, satisfy their social needs.

Wolves, wolf hybrids, and large dogs should not be allowed to roam free, except under special circumstances. If they unite in a pack, they are capable of bringing down large animals. The responsible owner should not allow this to happen. Enclosures should be soundly constructed to prevent escapes.

On the other hand, owners and animals alike can benefit from the pleasures of taking long hikes together. One should carefully monitor the circumstances of these outings, so that the animals can be kept under positive control. This will depend on the kind of training and discipline the hybrids have received. Disobedient animals are best left at home in their pens.

6

MYTHS

From time immemorial, wolves have been the objects of a deeply rooted fear, bordering on terror. Children's stories, such as "Little Red Riding Hood" and "Peter and the Wolf," implant fears and fantasies that seldom diminish as we grow older. In rural areas of the West, older citizens can recall the depredation of wolves on domestic livestock. Our contemporary newspapers carry accounts of wolves attacking people in distant Turkey and India.

Scientific studies of the wolf, begun in the twentieth century, and books by such writers as Farley Mowat and R. D. Lawrence, have done much to instill more positive images of *Canis lupus*. Indeed, the wolf now is admired by many for his dignity and courage, as well as for his habit of monogamy.

Of course, such an amiable view is not universal. Today's Navajo fear the wolf as werewolf and try to acquire white wolves to sacrifice for their skinwalking ceremony. The werewolf is "a person changed into a wolf or one capable of assuming the form of a wolf at will."* He haunts out there on the rimrock beyond the hogan, and strikes terror into people. Dorothy Prendergast writes that the "Navajo 'skinwalker' (is) not a werewolf. He is the 'bad medicine man'—[who] throws powdered drugs into the faces of his 'victims' to distort their perception and create fear. Around here they prefer the grey or grizzle-colored skins [to use in the ceremony]."**The late David Chethlahe Paladin, a renowned Navajo artist, wanted to acquire one of my white cubs, which he had no intention of sacrificing, because the "white wolf is in direct communication with the spirits."

Some western livestock growers continue to oppose suggestions that wolves be reintroduced into their native habitats, even if these releases would be carefully programmed. Hollywood and popular fiction still use wolf myth stereotypes to create dramatic effects at the expense of reality.

While a more accurate image of the wolf is gaining acceptance, the wolf hybrid is as yet poorly understood by many, among them, some of those who have successfully fought to place the wolf in a clearer light. They object to mixing the genes of a wolf with those of the "lowly" dog, a view to which, obviously, I do not subscribe.

Now let us look at some of the myths that burden wolves and wolf hybrids.

*Webster's New World Dictionary of the American Language, 2nd Ed., World Publishing Company, New York, 1970.
**Source: Personal communication.

The Wolf is/is Not Dangerous.

This is a myth with two contradictory versions. The first is that wild wolves are ferocious and dangerous to human beings. The second is that there has been not one instance of a wolf attacking a person in the wilds of North America.

The literature on the subject reveals that the interface between humans and wolves is quite different in North America from what it is in Europe, the Middle East and Asia. Serious human predation by wolves did take place in the British Isles and France until the animals were eliminated there, and in Portugal and Italy until their numbers were reduced. There are occasional reports of wolf attacks on humans in Turkey and India. Curiously, in India, there are also rare but credible reports of children being raised by wolves.

The situation in North America is quite different. During the Westward Expansion, trappers, explorers and other travellers frequently sighted wolves, and their recorded observations were not friendly. I have been able to uncover only three man/wolf encounters of a potentially hazardous nature in the nineteenth century. One involved a rabid wolf that wandered into a trappers' rendezvous. In another case, a man on horseback in Utah was chased by a pack of wolves at night. In the third instance, crusty old Uncle Dick Wooton reported a hand-to-paw fight to save his dogs from a rabid wolf.*

In the twentieth century, only three hostile encounters have been reported. (I do not number among these incidents those reported by Ernest Thompson Seton in

---

*See "From a Pioneer's Notebook," *Wolf Hybrid Times*, April, 1987.

Artic Prairies, because in those encounters the wolves were not threatening and only appeared to be curious about the explorers.) The most publicized attack took place in 1942, when a railroad worker riding an inspection car in Canada was attacked. The man was rescued and the wolf was thought to be rabid. In 1978, an Ojibway woman, Elsie Wolfe, who ironically was a member of the wolf clan, was found partly consumed by wolves. She was an epileptic and had been hiking home that winter night from her job as a camp cook. It is not known for certain whether she had been attacked by the wolves, had died from exposure, or had suffered an epileptic seizure. In 1982, a chap by the name of Ronald Poyirer scuffled with a wolf near Brimson, Minnesota. His clothes had been saturated with buck deer scent. Apparently it was a case of mistaken identity and Poyirer was able to resist the wolf's attentions.*

So we have six verified cases in two centuries. Undoubtedly there are others. But even if we multiply by a factor of ten, taking into account cases obscurely recorded and those unrecorded, and especially when we take note of the lack of deliberate hunting of human prey by wolves, as far as we know the wolf in North America can hardly be accused of posing a serious threat to man. Why this difference between North America and other areas where *Canis lupus* is found? One possible explanation lies in the vastness and remoteness of wolf habitats in North America, where the probability of encounters is less than in Europe or India. If this is the explanation, we can expect more

---

*For a description of this incident, and for some marvelous paintings of wolves, see the January, 1987 issue of *Audubon*, pp. 52-61, for an article by Jim Dale Vickery: "The Land Is Alive With Wolves."

incidents as human populations rise and as wolf habitats are reduced.

An alternative explanation may lie in the fact that the aggressive white explorers of North America were almost universally armed and hostile toward wildlife. Therefore they were more threatening to wolves than the unarmed peasants and villagers of India, Turkey or early Europe. This explanation, however, does not cover encounters with American Indians. It would not hold, for instance, if wolves did not commonly attack Indians in pre-contact times. Today, Indian tribes have widely divergent attitudes toward wolves and it appears that, in a general way, those tribes with greater historic contact with wolves are those that are less likely to fear them. This, if true, would not be surprising, given the human tendency to fear the unknown.

Wolves Stand Up to Howl, and Howl at the Moon.

Wolves can and do howl when trotting slowly, standing, sitting, or lying. I have not seen one howling while lying on his back with legs in the air but I would not rule out the possibility.

Artists' depictions of wolves and coyotes howling at a full moon are misleading. Wolves do *not* howl at the moon. Thank goodness! After all, a chap has to sleep! Of course howling does occur on moonlit nights, but the stimulus for vocalizing then is not different from what it is on other occasions.

Wolves and Wolf Hybrids Cannot Be Vaccinated Against Rabies.

This myth is one of the most serious, since some bureaucrats use it to justify banning wolf hybrids in their jurisdictions. Previously, wolves were not included in the testing programs that certified rabies vaccines for dogs. Although they are now, this does not yet preclude official seizures of privately owned wolves and wolf hybrids. Some owners bypass the problem by registering their animals as Malamute crosses. It would be irresponsible for owners not to vaccinate wolves and hybrids against rabies. Zoos and research organizations also do so, to protect their staff and the public.

Wolves and Wolf Hybrids Are Just Like Dogs.

Wolves, wolf hybrids and dogs are members of one family and share many physical and behavioral characteristics. Especially with regard to wolf hybrids, the differences may be subtle and not immediately obvious to persons unfamiliar with the animals. Dogs, however, do seem to recognize the differences. Many people who have purchased my hybrids comment that when their animals meet dogs, the latter become anxious and fearful and practice avoidance behavior. In the village of Cerrillos, New Mexico, passing dogs used to loudly challenge my fenced-in wolf hybrids. However, if one of the hybrids got loose it would be like a scene from *High Noon:* the dogs would immediately vanish from the scene.

For their part, wolf hybrids often are frustrated in their friendly overtures toward dogs. Wolf protocol—the necessary etiquette that allows a pack to function—is unfamiliar to dogs. So their meetings with the hybrids produces misunderstandings. It is as if two persons from widely different cultures — say a Moslem and a Maori — were confronting each other's foreign values and customs. The Moslem does not touch with his left hand, while the Maori will try to rub noses.

It should be apparent, at this point in my text, that wolves and wolf hybrids *are* different from dogs. It is this difference that many intelligent, responsible, sensitive people appreciate in them. But it is also why many other people should not own them. The unrecognized differences lead to other misconceptions that we will now explore.

The Eight to Ten Day Myth.

There is a school of thought that holds that wolves and wolf hybrids should be weaned from the mother eight to ten days after birth. The rationale is that mothers who are not socialized to human beings will transmit their fears to the cubs. This point of view is valid if applied to wild wolves or to captive wolves that have not been socialized. However, wolf hybrids that are comfortable with human beings will convey their acceptance of human friends to their cubs. This will be reinforced if the cubs are handled fondly by humans from an early age. As previously mentioned, the discipline cubs learn from their mother, father, uncles and aunts will make it easier for them to accept human discipline.

An equally important consideration, in avoiding early weaning, is physical health. Mother's milk provides a natural immunity from disease, and it is questionable whether formula substitutes can offer similar benefits.

As I have watched my wolf hybrids cycle in and out of

motherhood, I have become more sensitive to their profound attachment to their cubs, especially when the
cubs are very young. I have come to respect these feelings and prefer not to violate them.

The Breed of Dog Contributing to the Wolf Hybrid Mix is Unimportant.

In an article about wolves and wolf hybrids by
Christine Gentry, she claims that:

> It matters little if the young are descended from timber
> wolves, gray wolves or arctic wolves, whether they're
> mixed with German Shepherds or Malamutes (the two
> breeds most commonly used for crosses) or whether the
> proportions of wolf to dog are ¾ (three wolf grandparents),
> ½, ¼ or even ⅛ (one wolf great grandparent): Young wolf
> hybrids tend to resemble wolves in both physical appear-
> ance and temperament.*

Gentry is probably correct in asserting that the
subspecies of North American wolf will not signifi-
cantly influence the hybrid. But in her simple distinction she is mistaken about subspecies. The term "gray
wolf" does not properly refer to a subspecies but rather
allows a generic distinction to be made between the
southern red wolf and all other North American
wolves.

As discussed elsewhere, it may make a difference if
the wolf is crossed with German Shepherds or Malamutes. For example, temperamentally a German Shepherd may accentuate wolf characteristics that breeders
want to mute. But there are imponderables. Atsay, the
gentlest female in my pack, has German Shepherd on

---

*Christine Gentry, "A Pack of Trouble," *Dog Fancy Magazine*, p. 15. No
date or issue provided.

the dog side; but she is the only member of the pack to bark in nonthreatening situations. The Malamute's recurved tail is unwolflike and explains some breeders' preference for the German Shepherd. There are so many unknown elements in the huge gene pool from which the hybrids dip, that mechanistic judgments are unreliable. Look at the individual.

The reader may have noticed Gentry's error in calculating the manner in which wolf/dog proportions are computed. Different combinations of original numbers can lead to similar proportions. For instance, a ¾ wolf may have one parent who is pure wolf and another that is half wolf, or, perhaps more likely, parents each of whom were ¾ wolf.

Young Wolf Hybrids Are Easily Frightened and Sometimes Quite Aggressive.

Sometimes? Of course! This is true of dogs, as well. There is variation among wolf hybrids in a given litter and from litter to litter. Two of my litters born during the stress of a severe winter tended to exhibit fear reactions and were slow to become relaxed and sociable. Other litters from the same parents were very friendly and outgoing. Shy cubs from these litters eventually blossomed under the care of loving, patient, knowledgeable owners.

It is Impossible to Housebreak a Wolf or Wolf Hybrid.

Of course there are individual animals who learn this discipline only slowly. An older animal that has been outside all its life may achieve such control only with difficulty.

Housebreaking is a special case of the overall relationship of animal to owner and it is resolved best in the context of an animal loving the owner and respecting just discipline. Wolf cubs are naturally clean and early in their life learn to leave the denning area to eliminate. Even dogs show this tendency with their propensity to pop over to the neighbor's to poop.

Any Pet Wolf Will Eventually Come to a Head-to-Head Confrontation with its Owner Over who is Pack Leader.

There is a semantic problem here. "Any" and "will" imply that such confrontations will take place in all situations. R. D. Lawrence and Lois Crisler relate such challenges from their wolves, but none of the few pure wolf owners of my acquaintance have reported the problem. Neither have any wolf hybrid owners I have known. Nothing resembling a challenge to me for leadership by my animals has yet occurred, except for one or two who chose not to come when I called. I do not question the possibility of confrontations, but doubt that the incidence is significant.

7

WELL, NOBODY'S PERFECT!

The ownership of canids, large or small, carries with it a potential for problems. A small dog, for instance, might disturb a neighborhood if it yaps continuously. Nervous animals can injure people and, now and again, children are killed by larger dogs.

Fortunately, wolf hybrids rarely bark and, if they do, one should listen: it may mean that something is amiss. Their howling is another matter. To the owner, and many non-owners, the howling of a wolf can be a source of delight—a rare opportunity to make contact with something primordial. To close neighbors, particularly those not attuned to nature, the howling can be a bloody nuisance, especially if it is frequent. This underlines the fact that a rural atmosphere is more compatible with the ownership of wolf hybrids. Urban life is not to their liking. Neither is it harmonious for most of the people who yearn to own wolf hybrids.

The ownership of these animals may entail tradeoffs and sacrifices that many people would not accept. In particular, one must be home to feed them twice a day.

In this sequence, Chamaco is overwhelmed by the attentions of
two females and eventually tires of it.

Overnight trips or vacations are difficult to arrange, since wolf hybrids are especially unhappy if incarcerated in kennels. Finding a housesitter who is comfortable with them, and who has the confidence and experience to handle situations that might arise, is not easy. Such people are to be treasured. Since the wolf hybrid has a greater need for affection than do most dogs, the owner or owner-surrogate must enjoy spending time with them—sometimes quiet and sometimes boisterous times, that are always rewarding.

Special legal problems may arise with wolf hybrids. Some jurisdictions ban them. The grounds for these prohibitions vary. In some cases, they are considered wild, *ergo* dangerous. In others, there is the mistaken belief that wolves and wolf hybrids cannot be vaccinated against rabies. (However, even where laws and ordinances are exclusionary, they will not be enforced unless complaints are lodged.) Responsible ownership is necessary, not only in the interests of the individual pet, but also for the benefit of the wolf hybrid population as a whole.

As previously noted, large canids, whether dogs or wolf hybrids, should not be allowed to run free. The pack instinct is strong and the instinct to run down sheep, goats, horses and cattle is ingrained. They love to eat chickens, especially, but this problem can be solved if one ties a chicken the hybrid has killed around the perpetrator's neck and lets it rot there for a few days.

Wolf hybrids need exercise, for they are athletic animals. Several together in a large pen will frolic and chase, expending their energies harmlessly. They delight in hikes with their owners and can carry their own chow in canine backpacks. Purchasers of my animals report that they behave very well on the trail and that they receive many admiring comments from other hikers.

Housebreaking is sometimes a problem, although wolf hybrids are clean and, at a very early age, leave their denning area when they have to eliminate. One should look at housebreaking as a special case of discipline. If the animal is brought up from its earliest days in an atmosphere of benign order, it will soon learn the discipline of bowel control. Remember that its organs are small and do not have the capacity to hold waste for very long. Successful owners will watch their animals closely in the early stages and will put them outside often for short intervals, gradually lengthening their times inside.

Wolf hybrid cubs, like puppies, are energetic and curious. This, especially if they feel ignored or abandoned, can lead to destructive activity. Plan on this possibility and be prepared to deflect it in some way. If the cubs have the company of an older animal, their attention will be focused on this friend rather than on the furniture. They should not be left alone where temptation dwells. An outside pen and companionship are essential to avoid problems and to facilitate healthy transitions.

As noted above, wolf hybrids are natural landscape architects and mining engineers. In the summertime they will scrape shallow holes to get down to cool, moist dirt. Some enjoy digging under fences. Pregnant wolves will excavate long tunnels where their babies can be kept out of sight. If keeping an immaculate, formal garden is important to him, the wolf hybrid owner will have to allocate some out-of-the-way area for the pen. But to do so contravenes one of the advantages of having these animals—the pleasure derived from close contact.

Scent marking is important to wolf hybrids and shrubs don't always stand up well against such on-slaughts. When they are excited about exploring a new place, be it a forest trail or someone else's home, they will want to leave their "Kilroy was here" statement. Both males *and* females indulge in this behavior, although the females mark by half squatting and extending one leg forward, rather than sideways, as does the male—which, incidentally enables one to dis-tinguish the adult males and adult females in a pack from a distance. When a guest in someone's home, watch your animal closely, especially during the first few minutes after arriving.

Wolf hybrids are not passive bundles of fur. They are athletic, demonstrative animals who reward their owners richly, but only if they are the beneficiaries of loving care and understanding. People who do not have the time or inclination to give themselves to a pet should not own one, and this is especially true of the wolf hybrid. But if a commitment to a wolf hybrid is willingly made and carried through, the experience is sure to be profoundly enriching.

8

RAISING WOLF HYBRIDS: PROS AND CONS

There are several good reasons for raising wolf hybrids.

Sharing the Joys of Ownership with Others. Although now and again, as with humans, there are wolf hybrids with negative, disagreeable personalities, and now and again a poor match is made between hybrid and human, most owners are enthusiastic about their animals. They cart around photos to show the unwary, their eyes gleam with fervor, they relate endless tales of the delights of this companionship.

This is indeed the reason I plunged into the business and I have experienced few regrets. The warmth, the demonstrativeness, the sensitivity, the fascinating social behavior of wolf hybrids remain for me an enduring delight.

You Really Like People.
If people are not important to you, don't raise hybrids to sell because (a) you will meet a whale of a lot of people, and (b) the animals will sense how you feel about

visitors and the visitors, in their turn, will sense the chill from both you and the pack. Visitors will tend to show up at all hours, from dawn until after dark, at mealtimes, bath times, when work has to be done, and when one just feels like setting on the porch and whittling away at a stick. The people may have come from a long way away. At my ranch folks have dropped in from nearly every state, and from Canada, France, Spain, New Zealand, Mexico, Guatemala, Chile and Argentina. No matter how you feel at the moment, common courtesy demands that you make an effort, be attentive, answer questions and visit with them in a neighborly way. You may then reasonably expect that the guests will leave with warm feelings and with their understanding of wolves enhanced. And from these multitudes, you can be sure that some enduring friend-ships will be made. I have found that as I have come to understand and love wolves, so have I come to better understand and love people. It has been very worthwhile.

Hint: I *DO* have a lot of other work to do, so there is a notice posted near the entrance to the ranch emphasiz-ing: *NO MORNING APPOINTMENTS!* However, I hold open house every Sunday afternoon, when there sometimes are thirty or forty visitors. It can be difficult trying to respond to all the interest and to maintain hospitality as kids rush from pen to pen, poke little fingers through fences, climb over the furniture in dirty boots, leave doors open, want to go potty, and/or have a sodypop. I do not mean to imply that children are unwelcome: quite the contrary. But parents should control them carefully in a situation such as this.

You Want to Study Wolves, But Don't Feel Prepared for the Ownership of Pures.

Some persons are sceptical about the possibility of learning about pure wolves through studying wolf hybrids. As has been said, to best relate to wolf hybrids it is necessary to have some understanding of pures, since they have some important characteristics in common. One can learn a great deal from hybrids without having to deal with some of the special problems associated with pure wolves.

Ownership of pure wolves requires not only special permits, but expensive, escape-proof facilities. Pure wolves also are generally less tractable than hybrids, especially during mating season. And wolves cannot be taken out into the public as can hybrids.

Research into the social behavior of wolves raises a couple of questions for the breeder. One of these has to do with the number of animals in the pack. If close interaction with the animals is an important factor to you, the pack size should be limited to six or eight; otherwise it will not be possible to give them the time they need. And, if they are not properly socialized, problems can arise when they are in contact with other people. To the extent that the animals are socialized their pure lupine behavior is altered, and one must enter this *caveat* in interpreting what one observes.

There is also a conflict between a commercial breeding operation and research. Since usually only the *alpha* male and *alpha* female breed in the wild, the researcher would probably want to reproduce that situation; whereas the breeder would have several breeding pairs, in effect several mini packs. When natural conditions are altered, wolf behavior will alter accordingly. I have learned more from my wolf hybrids than from any other single factor in my life's experiences. This learning has resulted from informal observation rather than from disciplined study. The wolves challenge one to understand them, one's self, one's interactions with others, and the society of which we are a part. If one remains open to learning, and is prepared to modify and adjust his own perceptions and behavior, then the exchange with these animals can be greatly enriching.

Although much controversy surrounds wolves, public understanding is being enhanced. Responsible breeders and owners can play an important educational role, by avoiding conflicts with society at large and by setting proper examples. This is one of the reasons why a responsible owner prevents confrontations between his animals and livestock and household pets.

The breeder can contribute in more positive ways by allowing public access to his or her pack. The only wolves that most people see are those in zoos. In their confined quarters, these animals often appear surly and unattractive. How different are their meetings with wolves or wolf hybrids who enjoy human company, and demonstrate this pleasure with lively affection. This happy experience will linger in the visitor's consciousness for days after the encounter. It is hard to think of a better reason to own, or be owned by, wolves.

There are also several *poor* reasons for wanting to breed wolf hybrids:

You Want To Make a Buck.
I doubt that many breeders keep a full accounting of their expenses, some of which are obvious and are easily recorded. One usually knows the costs of fencing, advertising, feed and veterinarian's bills. But what about one's time? The yard-cleaning, the babysitting,

the training, the many hours spent with visitors? If the time spent on these tasks were recorded, a minimum wage would seem princely by comparison to what you earn. And there is what we economists call opportunity costs: the income that might have been earned by doing other things, but which is not earned because one is mucking out pens and talking to clients.

If you attempt to run a professional operation, it can be discouraging to be undercut by casual, backyard breeders who sell poor animals, sometimes at outrageous prices, and who care little about their future. Unfortunately there are many such operations, and bad breeders can drive out the good with such irresponsible practices as the following:

(1) No effort is made to qualify buyers, *i.e.* to ensure that buyers understand and accept the responsibilities of ownership and the unique character and sensitive nature of the hybrid.

(2) The animals are allowed to breed promiscuously and no effort is made to ensure the integrity of lineage. The animals cannot be registered and one has no way of knowing how much, if any, percentage of wolf is present. Misrepresentation of wolf lineage is a very common practice.

(3) The animals are undernourished and unhealthy. The cubs sold by one breeder I know of are frequently diseased; yet when they die, as many do, the buyers do not get their money back.

(4) The animals are allowed to run at liberty, to hunt and savage pets, domestic stock and wildlife.

(5) If pens exist, they are too small and not kept clean.

(6) Prices are often several times as high as those elsewhere in the market.

Horror stories abound concerning the treatment of animals and clients by unscrupulous breeders. Dishonest breeders tarnish the reputation of all breeders; and the poor state of their animals give wolf hybrids a bad name. It is next to impossible to earn a living raising wolf hybrids without engaging in ancillary practices. Some breeders train their animals for use in television commercials or in the film industry. This is a highly specialized trade requiring skill, time, dedication, and good connections, with room for only a few top professionals.

The "Just One Litter" Fallacy.

The conventional wisdom once held that the health of a female canid would be improved if she had a litter of pups before she was spayed. I do not feel myself qualified to comment with confidence on this, although the veterinarians with whom I have discussed it say that the contrary is true: that females should be spayed before their first heat for reasons of health.

Wolf hybrids, unlike pure wolves in the wild which have their first *estrus* at about twenty-two months, may come into heat when they are six to eight months of age. Since the hybrid continues to grow until about twenty months of age, the female will have her first heat while still an adolescent. A pregnancy at that age is not unlike what it can be for a high school teenager. Physiologically and psychologically, neither is prepared to undertake the responsibilities. And, not unlike the parents of human teenagers, the wolf hybrid owner does not have much control over which individual sires the litter. What if some Heinz-57 variety sneaks through the fence one day? What do you do with the progeny? Sell them? Give them away? Have them destroyed?

Teeth are not always used for aggression. Here, Chicha uses them to demonstrate affection.

The first pregnancy of a young canid is often traumatic and needs to be carefully monitored. An immature mother is less likely to care for the cubs adequately than a mature one. Futhermore, unless one is a professional breeder, one is unlikely to own other adult wolves whose role in the cub's learning process is very important. When someone talks of "letting" a young female "have just one litter," I wonder if they have weighed the advantages against the disadvantages. Before undertaking to become a breeder, give serious consideration to the points and arguments made in this chapter. If you are still enthusiastic, then go for it full throttle.

Some Other Factors to Consider.
What constitutes a professional approach to breeding?
The first requirement is to establish a long-term commitment, to be willing and able to withstand the vicis-
situdes that plague any endeavor, and to strive to maintain the highest standards of knowledge and ethics. Set
out to learn all you can about your new field of work.
Familiarity with publications such as those listed in
the *Suggestions for Further Reading* at the end of this
book are essential. The relevant professional organization is the United States Wolf Hybrid Association.
Membership provides access to information about
other professionals, and the opportunity to meet
owners and breeders and study their stock. Unfortunately, there is not as yet a breeders' association as
such, nor has a code of ethics for breeders been established.

The USWHA is considering a set of standards to
characterize the wolf hybrid. I am a little wary of this,
inasmuch as the highly restricted criteria used to
evaluate domestic breeds of dogs have led to the practice of emphasizing such physical features as conformation and color over matters of the animal's physical
and psychic health. The *spirit* of the wolf hybrid, one of
its most precious and endearing qualities, could be
overlooked in a concentration on physical features.

The breeder should make it his standard practice to
spend enough time with potential clients to evaluate
their suitability and to ease the transition to ownership. I look for sensitive, responsible people who
understand the limitations of ownership and who will
provide the animals with a healthy, loving
environment.

A high quality of stock clearly is important, but this

may take time to achieve—even, as in my case, several years. Until then, one should charge appropriate, rather than maximum, prices. From the buyers' point of view, as well as that of the cubs, it is desirable to keep the parents—as well as aunts, uncles, and grandparents, if possible—together on the premises. Outbreeding to an off-kennel stud makes it difficult for buyers to evaluate the future development of the progeny. It also, as has been said, denies the cubs the education and nurturing of their family.

Quality is enhanced by appropriate facilities: large, clean pens, secure and private dens, trees and shrubs for a natural setting, as well as sites from which the wolf can survey his world, are desirable. These things, as well as the loving care of the owner, will produce happy animals that will give delight to new owners.

Consider all these factors, and especially the time you will need to invest. Be prepared for visitors at all hours and be ready to receive them graciously, no matter how inconvenient it might be at any given moment. Whether the visitors buy is not necessarily as important as the impression of the wolf hybrid the visitor will take away from his visit to you, the dedicated professional caretaker and breeder.

9

IN THE CAUSE OF WOLVES

In an article in the December 1987 issue of *Outdoor Life*, the writer claimed to be quoting an "observer" who said, "Many who know wolves hate them; those who are ignorant of wolves love them."* Whoever this "observer" was, he got things backwards.

Wolves are hated only by those who fear them.

Earlier in these pages it was established that, in North America, wolves rarely pose a threat to human beings. Even though bears and mountain lions kill humans, they do not inspire the terror that some people feel when they hear the word "wolf." As far as wolves, lions and bears, as well as coyotes, are concerned, improperly protected livestock may be at hazard. In a study of wolf depredation in Minnesota, Steven Fritts reported, "From 1976 through 1980 the number of farms in the wolf range suffering unverified losses to wolves ranged from 9 to 19 ($\bar{x} = 13$) per year out of 12,230. From 1977

---

*Jim Zumbo, "Should We Cry Wolf?," *Outdoor Life*, December 1987, p. 50.

through 1980, the highest cattle losses claimed by farmers were 0.45 per 1,000 cattle available in 1979; the highest sheep losses claimed were 1.18 per 1,000 available in 1980."**

Fritts goes on to note that 66 percent of the total compensation for sheep losses went to *one* rancher in 1977, and another cattle rancher received 42 percent of the total compensation paid in one year and 51 percent in another. He also observes that poor animal husbandry practices, such as allowing calving to take place in brushy, remote areas, account for many losses. The point is that, despite the publicity of the occurrences, wolf depredation tends to be focused and manageable. Few persons would object to ranchers being compensated for losses through depredation, but, at the same time, the public has a right to demand proper animal husbandry practices, especially on multiple use public lands.

One of the things that happens when you get some notoriety in the media is that you receive a lot of mail. My article in the January, 1989 issue of *New Mexico Magazine* generated over eighty letters, to each of which I replied. Two of the letters originated with Belshaws previously unknown to me. An extended correspondence evolved with Wilbur Belshaw of Minnesota, who has had first-hand experience with wolves there. His comments are noteworthy.

> "Since we sold our cattle we don't see many sign anymore. They were a real problem when we first moved here but we learned that we had to calve early, so the calves would stay

**Steven H. Fritts, "Wolf Depredation on Livestock in Minnesota," U.S. Fish and Wildlife Service, Patuxent Wildlife Research Center, Laurel, Maryland 20708.

A family outing.

with their mothers when we turned them out to pasture. After that we had not real problem. Once in a while when we are on the road we see one. Some get up to 120-130 lbs."*

Over the years Hollywood has perpetuated some of the worst misinformation about wolves. Such films as "Never Cry Wolf," "Lobo," and "The Journey of Nattie Gann" present a more positive image, which still is not very accurate. However, they have served to generate some sympahty and a growing public interst, which is still better served by such books and articles as those I have recommended. These offer a fuller understanding of this interesting and intelligent animal, and its

*Personal correspondence quoted with Wilbur Belshaw's permission.

Parents keep a close watch over their cub

elaborate social structure, which also is environmentally beneficial in preventing destructive overpopulation among prey species. When predators are removed, as for example was the mountain lion from its range north of the Grand Canyon, ungulate populations proliferate, destroying the vegetation upon which they depend. The cycle is then reversed, as large numbers of herbivores die of starvation.

Those who truly know wolves, whether from research or through experience of its surrogate, the wolf hybrid, come to be impassioned advocates of wolf survival. So the wolf is gaining a constituency among those who urge that we oppose the blitzkrieg against American wildlife that began in the nineteenth century.

There is now public support and approval for efforts

Chamaco, the alpha male, leads the pack.

to reintroduce the Red Wolf in North Carolina, the
Mexican Lobo in the Southwest, and the Rocky Mountain Timber Wolf in Glacier National Park, Yellowstone National Park, and elsewhere. This ground-
swell, however, is opposed by special interest
organizations working to influence state governments
and local game and fish departments. At the federal
level, as this is written, the national leadership is
indifferent to environmental concerns.

The militant environmental advocacy of the 1960s
and '70s shocked us into recognition of the hazards of
indifference. But the complexities of these issues were
not recognized. We cannot advocate environmental
interests at all costs since the planet's resources are
finite. There must be a balance of interests. In the case
of the wolf, the rancher and the hunter line up against

those of us who want the wolf to survive, especially on those public lands that belong to us all.

Responsible organizations such as Defenders of Wildlife and the National Audubon Society understand this. But we also need strong state and local support for preservation of the natural world, to balance but not negate other interests. It is here that, so far, we have failed.

10

EPISODE IN THE FORM OF AN EPILOGUE

If our lives have meaning, we are always passing through some kind of transition, from a way station that was once a goal towards a goal that will become a way station. For most of my life, my chosen way was to be an integral part of range upon range of noble mountains. Deserts seemed to me to be harsh, inhospitable and cruel. Life in Arizona changed that somewhat and the mountain man became a desert rat, awed by the stark and sere silhouettes of cactus–clad mesas. Yet the high peaks of New Mexico beckoned the wolves, and the Spanish villages their leader. The proximity to relatively unspoiled nature and a warm, vibrant culture were irresistible, and I purchased a ranch in a place where the Rocky Mountains fold themselves into the magical multicolored buttes so well understood and interpreted by Georgia O'Keeffe. The ranch, an abandoned homestead, is what is known as a Forest Service inholding, that is, a tract of land completely surrounded by National Forest, and thereby protected from development. Here my wolves can howl to their soul's delight.

If you clamber up one of the mesas or granite mountains on the ranch, primitive and unspoiled vistas unfold, mysterious hills, mesas, buttes, *llanos* and canyons stretch forty miles to the distant, snowcapped Sangre de Cristo Mountains. Enough to bring tears to the eyes of a grown man. It is a wonderful place for the man-related wolves as well, for wild wolves, too. If the grown man has a practical as well as a poetic bent, the land holds real treasures—sand and adobe soils to build with, stone and virgin ponderosa for log cabins, too. But imagine a time when no buildings at all were there. The homesteader's cabin has been torn down long ago. The spring is clogged with silt and has gone underground. The wolves and their leader cannot easily hold out against the unforgiving snows, without shelter and water. So the man finds a traditional adobe house that he can rent, tucked away in an apple orchard on the edge of a village nearby. He wonders how the wolves will fare in this farming community, where the water flows into the *acequias* each spring to irrigate pasture and crops and cattle and sheep meander through high mountain meadows. In this place, wolves once menaced the stock of ancestral kinfolk, and I knew that those losses were remembered and some of the fears remained. Of nearby Tres Piedras, Elliott Barker wrote:

> "In the side of Bald Wind Mountain we found where they had been while it was snowing. We found the tracks and soon came upon the worst bloody mess I have ever seen. An old wolf bitch and two nearly grown ones had found the sheep and killed, or mortally wounded, eighty-seven of

them. A number were left alive, their flanks ripped open
and entrails dragging. At the end of the killing spree, they
had eaten from three carcasses, while the others had been
killed for fun."*

I brought my wolf hybrids to the village slowly, over a
period of a month, and installed them in large, portable
pens from which they could not see the outside world
and from which they could not be seen. The "outside
world" consisted of houses some hundreds of yards
away, cattle and horses in pastures and, in spring and
early summer, men cleaning the *acequias* and irrigat-
ing the fields. My own outside contacts, also, were few.

One day the *mayordomo* of the *acequia* knocked at
my door to tell me not to be concerned if I should see
him about his tasks before the dawn. Later he became a
treasured friend. Of course, the presence of my wolves
could not be completely concealed. They announced
themselves often during the days and nights. I gritted
my teeth and waited.

Then a man who lived a mile away told me that his
little girl was talking proudly of "her wolves." A young
boy had said, "Golly! I can't go to sleep at night until
the wolves sing me a song." Gradually the children
overcame their timidity, drifting by in small groups.
They were always polite and sensitive, asking intelligent questions and listening carefully to my responses.
When Fantasma, a pretty white wolf, died the night of
her birthing travail, I was touched by their expressions
of grief. Soon the parents started to visit with their
children. One of them said to me, "We are going to
miss the wolves when you move to the ranch." Another
told me, "Since your wolves came here the coyotes

* Elliot S. Barker, The Great Southwest, Lowell Press, Kansas City, Mis-
souri, 1974, p. 120.

have not attacked our sheep. Last year they came in broad daylight! The coyotes must be warned off by the wolf songs."

"Ai! What beautiful animals they are," I heard more than once. Cattlemen and hunters brought the wolves treats of fat and bones. This personal story, it seems to me, is testimony to a profound and healthy change in America regarding the natural world and our place within it. Through much of the nineteenth and twentieth centuries we were driven to overpower and dominate nature. The rivers were to be dammed and rechanneled. Mountains were obstacles that gave way to railroad tunnels and superhighways. Fields were to be irrigated and swamps drained. Animals that got in our way were thoughtlessly destroyed. We were vital, full of energy, and arrogant. Now, we are beginning to learn to live in harmony with nature. This new orientation, reinforced by the schools and the media, has evolved from the recognition of the harm we have wrought upon our irreplaceable wilderness and the life it harbors. My personal witness to this encouraging change of mind is that, even in such tiny and isolated enclaves of rural America as I have described, wolves, once so hated and feared, are gaining acceptance and a chance to live undisturbed.

Wolf hybrids are deeply attached to their owners. Here, Sitka complains loudly when he is left behind.

APPENDIX A: Summary of Observations for the Wolf Hybrid Owner

Choosing the Cub
1. Buy from a breeder with good facilities and a professional attitude.
2. Do the animals, adults and cubs, appear happy, healthy and alert?
3. Are the parents on the premises?
4. Select, as well as you can, on the basis of disposition.
5. Do not overemphasize color. It will probably change.
6. Do not overemphasize size as a criterion.

Living with the Wolf Hybrid
1. Read and observe all you can about wolves, but be skeptical of movies and some of the more popular books.
2. Provide the animal with companionship, for it is highly social and this need must be fulfilled.
3. Do *not* leave a wolf hybrid home alone on a regular basis, while you are off to work.
4. When the wolf hybrid is not with you, provide it and its animal buddies with a comfortable, clean, large and escape-proof pen.

5. Do not let the wolf hybrid or other large dog run free.

6. Be the *alpha* of your pack, but do not be harsh or arbitrary.

7. Wolf hybrids are sensitive animals. Be patient and tactful with them.

8. Wolf hybrids are athletes. Let them have plenty of exercise.

9. Above all, accept with joy the long-term nature of your commitment to the wolf hybrid.

APPENDIX B: Current Status of the Southern Rocky Mountain Wolf in the Southwest: Report of Research in Progress

Persons owning wolf hybrids are naturally concerned about the condition of wild wolves in North America and follow closely such issues as reintroduction efforts in Yellowstone, the Red Wolves in Cape Romaine National Wildlife Refuge in South Carolina, and the land and shoot hunting practices in Alaska. In the Southwest, controversy surrounds the as-yet-unsuccessful effort to reestablish the Mexican wolf, *Canis lupus baileyi*, exists in the Four Corners region of Arizona, Colorado, New Mexico and Utah. These animals were thought to be extirpated in the 1930s. However, the author heard undocumented reports of wolf sightings before he moved to New Mexico in 1983 and in 1987 saw a light-colored canid, clearly resembling a wolf, stalking sheep in a canyon pasture. This prompted him to begin a more formal survey of sightings using a form adapted from that used to report sightings in the northern Rocky Mountain states.

The author makes a practice of querying persons who, in their various capacities, might have encountered wolves. As of May 1990 some thirty possible sightings or other signs were recorded, covering the years from 1936 to 1990 but clustered in the late 1980s. The majority of the sightings were made by persons qualified to distinguish wolves from either dogs or coyotes by reason of professional training or extensive experience with wildlife. Ten were made by hunters or fishermen, five were made by sheep or cattle ranchers, four by foresters or loggers, and two by professional naturalists. Seven of the sightings were of light-colored animals which predominated among the *Canis lupus youngi* reported by Young and Goldman.* In one case, a cast of a paw print, 5" by 4½" was made. Most encounters were extremely brief—on the order of ten seconds or less—but observers were instantly impressed by the size of the animal and the intense stare as it turned to look at the intruder before disappearing.

It would seem that there is a small, but viable, population of Southern Rocky Mountain wolves in the Southwest. However, there are four unsubstantiated reports of animals being shot and a small population could be killed by humans or decimated by disease such as parvo, and eliminated forever. For this reason, there is some urgency to this continuing research which will, it is hoped, lead to better protection.

The author would be glad to share his information with qualified individuals, and requests that persons who believe that they may have seen a wolf in the Southwestern states at some time during the last five decades, contact him:

Michael Belshaw, Ph.D.
c/o Red Crane Books
826 Camino De Monte Rey
Santa Fe, NM 87501

*Stanley P. Young and Edward A. Golman, *The Wolves of North America*, Dover Publications, N.Y.

SUGGESTIONS FOR
FURTHER READING

Books
Durward Allen, *Wolves of the Minong*, Houghton Mifflin, Boston, 1979.

David Brown, Ed., *The Wolf of the Southwest,* University of Arizona Press, Tucson, 1983.

Edward Hoagland, *Red Wolves and Black Bears,* Penguin, East Rutherford, N.J., 1983.

R. D. Lawrence, *The North Runner,* Ballentine, N.Y., 1980.

——————, *Secret Go the Wolves,* Holt, Rinehart and Winston, N.Y., 1980.

——————, *In Praise of Wolves,* Henry Holt, New York, 1980.

David Mech, *The Wolf,* Natural History Press, Garden City, N.Y., 1970.

The Monks of New Skete, *How to Be Your Dog's Best Friend: A Training Manual for Dog Owners*, Little, Brown & Co., Boston, 1978.

Adolph Mutie, *The Wolves of Mount McKinley,* University of Washington Press, n.d.

Roger Peters, *Dance of the Wolves,* Ballentine, N.Y., 1985.

Dorothy Prendergast, *The Wolf Hybrid,* 2nd Edition, Rudelhaus Enterprises, Gallup, 1989.

Hope Ryden, *God's Dog: A Celebration of the North American Coyote*, Penguin Books, Middlesex, 1979.

Ernie Smith, *Warm Hearts and Cold Noses,* Sunstone
Press, Santa Fe, 1987.

Erik Zimen, *The Wolf—His Place in the Natural
World,* Souvenir Press, London, 1981.

Periodicals

Jim Dale Vickery, "The La..........
Audubon, Vol. 8...

United S...

Wo...

Wol...
14...

Wolve...
9130...